A Five Time Cancer Survivor

His Grace Made Me Whole

A Five Time Cancer Survivor

His Grace Made Me Whole

By

LTC (Retired) Shatrece W. Buchanan

Unless otherwise indicated, Scripture quotations are from the New King James Version of the Bible.

Published by
Laval Dreams, LLC.
8549 Wilshire Blvd, Suite #1442
Beverly Hills, California, 90211
www.LavalDreams.com

ISBN 978-0-692-63289-5

Printed in the United States of America
Edited by Dr. Lorraine Williams, M.D., M.P.H.
Author's website: www.eagletalon.org

Dedication

I would like to dedicate "A Five Time Cancer Survivor" first to My Lord and Savior for governing and preserving my life so that I would live to tell this story.

Second, I dedicate this book to anyone who has been struck by the hand of cancer. Though afflicted, we are not defeated.

If affected directly or indirectly, I dedicate this book to you, as a gift of encouragement.

And to those who have returned home-heaven bound, this book is written to remember and to honor your life.

To Uncle Ray, Harvey Sr., Heidi, Katie, Lydia,

Mr. George, Ronnie, Porscha-rest well.

To those enduring-hold strong to Faith in our Father.

Contents

Forward

by Donald Yance, MH, CN

I am a Clinical Herbalist and Certified Nutritionist, as well as member of the Secular Franciscan Order (also referred to as Third Order Franciscan. I have developed a personalized, integrative model referred to as the Eclectic Triphasic Medical System (ETMS), also sometimes referred to as "Mederi Medicine," with a special focus in Oncology.

When I first consulted with Shatrece, she was very ill with advanced metastatic breast cancer and her doctors had run out of options. I told Shatrece, as I tell all of the people I work with, I would do everything in my power to get her well and keep her well, now she must do the same, as well as any other relative partners in her health journey, and the rest we would leave in God's hands and trust that we would always be cared for no matter what. I encouraged her not to worry or project any negative beliefs about her situation, no matter what she was told. I have seen more often than not, people get well that nobody ever thought had a chance, and I firmly believed there was hope for Shatrece. Hope includes all the psychological advantages of optimism, but it is rooted in something deeper. The words of Naomi Remen, M.D. a nationally recognized physician and educator, echo this: "Perhaps the most basic skill of the physician is the ability to have comfort with uncertainty, to recognize with humility the uncertainty inherent in all situations, to be open to the ever-present possibility of the surprising, the mysterious, and even the holy, and to meet people there."

As you will find in reading this book, the ETMS practiced at the Mederi Centre for Natural Healing, includes the careful study of modern scientific literature. However, it does not sacrifice wisdom for the pursuit of knowledge. Wisdom differs greatly from knowledge. Wisdom begins in faith, is developed through rational understanding and time, and is perfected by the mystical union with God.

I have humbly discovered in my twenty-five+ years of clinical practice that nothing in medicine works automatically, no matter how technologically advanced we become. The Spirit (theology) must embody the mind (mentality), for the mind cannot heal without the spirit, and the spirit employs the mind in the quest to heal.

As you read Shatrece's book, you will be moved and inspired by her deep faith, inner strength, and ability to navigate the reality of the standard-of-care in the oncology world today, which so many face. Shatrece was given an extensive ETMS protocol consisting of botanical and nutritional formulations that focused on first, strengthening her own innate healing capacity, second, altering the microenvironment (based on numerous blood tests), to make it the most conducive to vibrant health, and the least conducive to cancer, and third, targeting the "phenotype" or personality and specific characteristics of her cancer.

As Shatrece mentions, this protocol is not for the faint of heart and requires a deep commitment to "stay the course" for an extended period of time. In addition to a comprehensive natural protocol, it also involves a lot of investigation to identify various tumor biomarkers that provide specific clues for determining the best potential drug therapies. Of course this is difficult to achieve without the support of a cooperative physician who is willing to collaborate and be open to recommendations outside of their area of expertise. Also, without the training to understand the relevance and interpret the findings in order to recommend the appropriate treatment, there are real liabilities. I have trained many complementary physicians who often struggle with the limitations of oncology today who purely have the best interest of the patient at heart and know there are better options for improving patients' quality of life, and patients are beginning to realize this struggle as well.

The "5X cancer survivor book" goes way beyond a book about surviving advanced stage breast cancer, but is a book about thriving and living. For we have already survived as believers and this is not a book on survival tactics as much as it is a testament of faith and the pursuit of truth, together with beauty and love. It is also a wonderful personal account of the intimate journey through the cancer world of today. I was very moved and touched by Shatrece's story, and I believe readers will find great strength and courage through her words and the spirit by which she has written them. I believe there are only two kinds of people in this world—those who are alive and those who are afraid. Shatrece is alive and well as you will hear her declare throughout this book. I believe this is to a great extent because she chose love over fear.

Albert Einstein said: "There are two ways to live: you can live as if nothing is a miracle; and you can live as if everything is a miracle." This has always been one of my favorite quotes. For me, it is a beautiful reminder that spirit is always present. I consciously pay attention to the miracles that are so abundant in everyday life, including the miracles in the healing work that I am called to do. Shatrece is one of those miracles that inspires me to make a difference in the lives of others every day.

Donald Yance,MH,CN
MederiFoundation
MederiCentre for Natural Healing
Ashland, Oregon, 97520
541.488.6949

Introduction

The year is 2015. The New Year has just arrived. It is 1:55 am... and I dedicate my first words to my Lord and Savior, who gave me the finished works of healing, as one of my many blessings. He revealed himself to me, to encourage me with signs and multiple words of support from my family, friends and even strangers. *He has continually demonstrated that the devil could not have my life..."not so" said the Lord, "not so"!*

I want to extend a special thanks to my family for their unwavering support through my journey. To my husband-Harvey, thank you for your patience and love. I appreciate your being there for the many doctors' appointments and all of the sacrifices you have made while I was on my road to recovery. To mom-Ingrid Sherfield, grandmother- Mayola Robinson, aunt Pamela Marshal, uncle Bob Marshal, and my Bryant family: Bobby, Robyn, Amy, uncles Willie, Larry, Alvin, and Wilbert; and my aunts Goldie, Brenda, Emily, and Shirley and family; aunts Ann Biery and Sharon Ashley; Thalaya Mathis, Arthur Ray and Kathy Parker, Angel and Dameron Batson, cousin Barbara Green, Jerry Buchanan, Harvey Sr. and Morristeen Buchanan...I thank each of you for your love, the long talks, the crying, the fussing, and most importantly, I thank you for your affirming words and prayers.

To my close friends...there are too many to name, but I would be remiss if I did not thank Charles McDonald Sr., my sounding board and spiritual/business battle. To Tina Marie Barnes and Shirley Stephens, my advocates who patiently paid attention to all of the nitpicky details of my care. To Vicki Johnson, Sharon

Buntin, and Deborah Brown.. my New Jersey, New York and Detroit girls....I could not have asked for a better love/support system. To Master Sergeant Robert Smith, my real life war battle partner, who praised the Lord with me and allowed me to be a soldier, yet human-crying tears of agony in private, while publicly serving our country dutifully in a foreign, war-struck country.

To all my new friends from every hospital and clinic; the doctors, nurses, volunteers and fellow patients, I thank you all. I thank each of you, for your role in the Master's plan. I send a special acknowledgment to the Mederi Centre for Natural Healing in Ashland, Oregon. Mederi was a saving grace from God to me, a place I believe that every patient with cancer and treating physician should experience. I would also like to acknowledge Dr. Ansanelli and staff from the Laser Breast Cancer Surgery Center, Plainview, New York. There are so many more angels who helped me along the way. May God bless all those who have also run this race fighting their way through. To those who have gone on to glory; Ingrid Sherfield, Mayola Robinson, Harvey Buchanan Sr, uncle Major General Alvin Bryant, Heidi Marshall, Katie Bell, Albert George- thank you all for your inspiration as you fought with dignity!

I would also like to thank both my spiritual advisors: Apostle Hubert McDonald for giving me the first warning signal from the Lord, as well as the second signal that has sustained me to this day; and to Minister Laval Belle, thank you for relaying the specific instructions for me to write this book, and thank you for keeping me doggedly focused.

Thank you Lord for the last ten years with my canine angel Porsha Jade who stood with me through it all, and then with strength and dignity went to heaven on Jan 4th, 2015 at 0345am riddled with lymphoma.

Who am I? I am Shatrece Buchanan, currently serving in the army of the Lord, and a retired Lieutenant Colonel of the United States Army. Now please, join with me as I tell you my story as a 5(x)time cancer survivor!

Chapter 1

Divine Signals and Instructions

The Background:

The year was 2005. I had just finished a grueling but rewarding year at the prestigious Command General Staff College in Leavenworth, Kansas. My class was the last official class where the top candidates had to face a rigorous selection process for entrance. My acceptance into the school and the previous promotion to Major, all in itself were one of God's setups. My promotion to Major was a serious blessing. The first time around, I was not selected and this usually meant that future promotions would be slim to none, let alone getting selected into Command General Staff College. I believe this was one of the clearest times in my life where I shifted my approach to a life of faith. This approach required me to apply specific scriptures to something I wanted, and I would speak it into manifestation. This was also a specific time in my life where I remember humbling myself before God saying, *"Not my will, but yours."* I released all of me to him saying, *"Lord, if I have to lose it all, then so be it."* I remember talking as well to two of my military colleagues who were also passed over for promotions and who both felt humiliated and rejected from a system they had poured most of their adult lives into. Our circumstances were similar, our experiences would be different. By observing them, I experienced an empowerment of sorts, as I rediscovered this gift of faith, and as I walked in and developed it. This faith naturally surfaced in other aspects of my daily life. For example, in my monthly coaching and mentoring sessions with my other military colleagues, I would not let them give up. We just could not give up.

For God has not given me a spirit of fear, but of power and of love and of a sound mind ...
2Timothy 1:7 (NKJV)

It was at this time that I began to notice my growth and who I was becoming in the Lord. Not getting promoted the first time around was like getting the kiss of humiliation in front of all my peers, family and friends. So, the way I responded made all the difference. I could yield to man's expectations and their negative words and unjustified claims, or I could believe God and his promises for me. So there it was. The military never could challenge my work ethic, the quality of my work, nor could they challenge my character. Throughout my career and those valley times of serious challenge, I often wondered...*why did I have to face so many unwarranted challenges? Was it because I was a woman? Was it because I was African-American? Was it because of my personality? What exactly was it Lord?* - I often questioned.

As I often reflected on these questions, I am reminded of a particular Colonel from a previous assignment who was in his mid 50's. Yes, this is called a flashback in time.

I will soon get back to year 2005. This particular Colonel had been my boss. I was originally hired to work for a two-star equivalent civilian in the District of Columbia metropolitan area for a particular top governmental agency. But because the Colonel did not like blacks advancing, by his own admission to me, he prevented me from not only working for several of the key blacks in the building, and he blocked me from working for any of the other esteemed leaders. At that time, this agency was home to the highest ranking African-American logistics' General and many other senior ranking military individuals. So I asked this Colonel, "why are you blocking me from advancing"? He responded by saying that he wished that he had a hundred leaders like me as he reflected on my work ethic, but he also had one major problem with me. He said, and I am paraphrasing, "because of your faith, you will never succeed in an organization like this. Your faith is too strong and you would never be able to objectively lead troops and make good decisions for others because your views are skewed. People like you, who have such faith, only belong in religious institutions." As a young Captain sitting in a counseling session with my boss, I held my ground to this jaded eagle. My boss further asserted, and in retrospect actually threatened me by saying that "I was never to go upstairs alone with the black or white Generals because they would hire me in a minute because I was a pretty black woman." He also forbade me from wearing a skirt as part of my military uniform. And lastly for that counseling session, he told me if I disregarded his directions, he would creatively prevent my advancement. As a young Captain, I knew something was awry. I knew it didn't feel right, it didn't taste right, it certainly didn't sound right within my core. Who knew at such a young age that I would have such an intimate association with discrimination, racial, religious and gender all at once. This too was one of God's setups, as 15 years later, I would hold a key position in a major command staving off the same ills of the human heart against freedom of religion, freedom against gender and racial discrimination? Who knew? I am certain now the adversary was in full pursuit from the very beginning. He saw my destiny before I did. That sucker!

"But God who began a good work in me,
is faithful to complete it...
Philippians 1:6 (NKJV)

And so it was- a long awaited answer. As I pondered all the questions of why there were so many trials and tribulations, I have now come to the realization, that my faith has always been under attack. And in consistent fashion, this has been the story of my life. This really is the story of every Christian's life, the enemy attacks constantly. For he knows that if we believe, trust and hope in the Lord, we will live in total victory. His goal therefore is to keep us frustrated and living in fear. For fear is the antithesis of faith. That is why Paul urged Timothy in ***1 Timothy 1:19 (NKJV):***

"to hold fast to faith and good conscience that his life might not be shipwrecked or diverted."

So back to 2005, where the Lord had miraculously blessed me to complete a school that only the top military leaders attend. After consulting with my husband, I decided to take a command in the Kansas city region to allow the family time to reconcile during this three-year assignment. Those three years were the best of times and the worst of times. I was blessed to be able to lead an organization with integrity and excellence. While there were similar challenges in the ranks to block my advancement and mission, I walked into this setting with a greater faith and better understanding and knowledge of how to handle these seemingly natural attacks which really were spiritual attacks.

For it is true that we wrestle not against flesh and blood but against principalities, against powers...
Ephesians 6:2 (NKJV)

Within the first ninety days, I knew who my enemies were and I knew that I had to have a battle plan. The enemy was strong, but I committed to standing on God's Word. His Word says, **be strong and of good courage...God would never leave me, nor forsake me... Deuteronomy 31:6 (NKJV)** and I am confident of this very thing that **he who has begun a good work in me will be faithful to complete it...Philippians 1:6 (NKJV).** So during this time period, I decided to put a spiritual battle plan together. First, I joined in agreement with my pastor and his wife, Pastor Kenneth and Katina White. The church had intercessory prayer on Saturdays, so I decided to go there and commit to an hour of prayer to pray for strength to deal with my enemy. I knew it would be a long three years, and when I tell you I was tried at every level..I was tried. It was clear the powers to be did not want me there. The good news is that it made me work feverishly to ensure I did everything with excellence and certainly above board all the way to the end. As our command tour was ending, I had to make a decision about a senior ranking enlisted marine who failed to do his job consistently and who put troops in danger. In this case, the marine was seriously derelict and refused to improve after constant assistance. A time came when I had to make a decision and reflect on the gentleman's flagrant disregard for professionalism in performing his assigned work. As a result, I had to rate him adversely on a performance report. My boss was a senior ranking Marine and believed in protecting his Marines, even a Marine who endangered others and did not do his job. In a nutshell, because I refused to change my report, the senior officials decided to end my career. God blessed me anyway to earn the next rank of Lieutenant Colonel(LTC). However, I knew that based on the previous actions of the chain of command, I would not be allowed to advance to the ranks of Colonel or General. I made the decision anyway knowing that LTC would be where I would stop in man's army.

Encouragement point: Now, as you listen to all of this... know this...the devil does not play fairly. Just as God has a destiny and a plan for you to succeed and to prosper, **the adversary-the thief comes to steal, to kill and to destroy (John 10:10, NKJV).** He does not play fairly because he knows your destiny too. And when you get attacked like this, you must stop and tell yourself to press forward, for there is something great in your future. My life is an example of this....you are reading this book because I chose to press forward through the perpetual attacks to get to you, to encourage you.

It is now 2008, and I am preparing to leave the command after three long grueling years of attack. The chain of command was so shocked that I got promoted to LTC, they continued their sentiments and comments, "we will write a report and make it so that she never sees Colonel or General. There is something about her that we cannot allow to advance." And so I believed that at the end of this particular three year tour, that I had endured the very worst. Through the incessant attacks on my job, my character, my work ethic...it had been more than tough....it had been often unbearable and humiliating....but I consistently held my head up and took the hits.

Every day, I would tell my faithful employees, "Watch the Lord. He will prevail. Lies and deceit cannot beat God's plan for us. God is bigger than any ill-guided colleague, or drunk/racist/confused boss." I was a soldier in the United States army. Despite the attacks, I had remained focused on the mission at hand. My approach to the attacks was to maintain my spiritual ground by any means and hold on to God's word at whatever cost. But God didn't let it end the way they had desired-in disgrace. It ended like this: first the promotion to Lieutenant Colonel; second, a very honorable change of command; and then another promotion as Discrimination Advisor in a two-star division.. Wow, what an awesome God. I was continuously grateful. And there were still more blessings coming. After the storm, a period of calm came. I had applied for the Advisor position because I wanted to learn more about discrimination law, after all, I had experienced it firsthand. I knew how it tasted, I knew how it smelled, I knew its texture and its character, but I just didn't know how to beat it, and I didn't yet know its full name. The decision to accept this position placed me with orders to go to Cocoa Beach, Florida, to the only defense race relations school in the US - the **Defense Equal Opportunity Management Institute** (DEOMI).

The First Time Around:

Prior to leaving, my new spiritual leader and advisor, apostle Hubert McDonald called me to preach at his church and then invited me again for our final meeting to speak a word to me. After the sermon that particular day, the Lord told me to gather all the women in the church and to pray over them. The Lord said, "just don't pray for them, hug them, love them and bear their burdens. Hug them and over embrace them. As you do this, sing just these words into their spirit....*wrap your arms around me, Lord, wrap your arms around me Lord, wrap your arms around me Lord and nurture me*....this song was sung by Shekinah Glory and the Lord wanted me to sing that while praying, hugging and bearing all that was within. I remember immediately afterwards, I left the service with the hottest hands. They stayed hot at least 5 days or so following. It was odd to me. I knew something had happened in the spirit...I just didn't understand it. Over six years later, I learned that was the fire of the Holy Spirit. I do remember though, asking the Lord before the service...if this is what you want me to do, then will I get sick from absorbing the load of others? So to those of you wondering, oh my, she asked that question...yes, I did.

About one month after that service, my family was positioned to relocate from the Kansas city area. My Apostle asked me to come to another service for a final farewell. During that service my advisor asked me to accept a word he had gotten from the Lord. I stood up in front of a crowd of at least seventy five people in a small church, and he said the following:

> "In a little while, you will transition from this place. During your transition, you will go through one of the greatest trials in your life. 'You are to stand firm,' says the Lord 'because the enemy wants your life', but the Lord says, 'Not so'."

Ok, was this a warning signal? And were these instructions?

I stood there in front of the crowd speechless. Should I have said, thank you Apostle! What a great word or should I have said, thank you for the heads up. Frankly, I didn't know what to think, say or do. I do remember thinking to myself, now what kind of trial can he be talking about? It can't be anything more than the trial I had just endured for the last three years on my the job. I had never endured such persecution before...he must be referring to that...he must.

I had just a few weeks left in the area and was at the house dealing with the movers and that's when I found it. It just appeared out of nowhere it seemed. It was a very real presence that said, pay attention to me. I am here. I ignored it for days, thinking that somehow it would go away, but the lump was persistent. My first thought was the worse. That lasted 2seconds, and I made myself go another way, think another way. After all, my recent mammogram had been normal. The first week passed...and the mass on my right breast, near the underarm would not leave. After the second week, I mentioned it to my husband. He heard me, but he didn't. Maybe he thought the same as I had done-this is just something she has observed, and it will pass. Little did he know, little did I know. Nothing else was said about it at that point. So on my last day on my job, I said goodbye to everyone, but there was one person who I needed to talk to in a pressing way. That was Mr. Albert George.

Mr. George was a cancer survivor, and I had watched him for over two years work through his journey. Mr. George had worked with me in the headquarters, as my budget technician. I had worked hard to get this 65-year-old, marine veteran and former local businessman on my direct staff. Every day he loved. Every day he encouraged. Every day he came to work with a spirit of thankfulness. He was an angel in disguise. That day, I decided to confront my worse fear. I sat down on that last day in a closed-room setting, and I said, "Mr. George, I must tell someone who will listen." He asked ma'am, "what is it"?. I then told him, "I found a lump on my right breast." He first looked at me quietly. I bowed my head, tearing up. I could not let him see his Commander cry, but he knew, and he took my hand and softly said, "you know what you have to do. Go to the doctor and do not keep this inside any longer." That was the word of the year.

In July 2008, my family and I moved to Georgia. We immediately got the household set up and son registered in school. My husband and son would stay in Georgia without me for 3 months while I attended DEOMI....the race relations school for certification. Through the long travel from Kansas to Georgia...I said nothing about the new development in my life. For the time, I had tucked it away...I said I would get to it when I slowed down. In my mind, you see, the Lord had blessed me with a very prestigious job and I had to prepare for it. I would be serving as the advisor to a commanding general...wow. I had no time to think about new developments in my body. Perhaps what I felt and saw would just go away. So, I buried it and went to Florida for my training.

When I arrived in Cocoa Beach, Florida, the school was surrounded completely by water. If there is one thing I love, it is being around water-on a beach or a lake. I was truly in paradise. I was however there to work on assignment, to get certified to work as an advisor in my new specialty.

I began the rigorous program and worked with a certain feverish resolve. Others could not understand my passion. I eagerly wanted to know everything about discrimination law. I was angry that I had worked all these years for a bunch of 'you know whats' who had preemptively decided to change the course of my career. This was a hard pill to swallow. Although I had been promoted to a Lieutenant Colonel, I knew I would have to work with peers for the next three years and then watch them go on to the next level without me. I was angry because I knew within myself that I was certainly capable of being a full bird Colonel or General. Within myself I knew and still know, that God had set me apart to be a leader to the nations. I recall -

> ***Before you were formed in your mother's womb,***
> ***I knew you. Before you were born, I set you apart,***
> ***I appointed you as a prophet to the nations...***
>
> **Jeremiah 1:5 (NKJV)**

Now, years before my mentor had drilled this into me. I knew that I was set apart and was uniquely made to lead, to influence and to teach God's principles. As a result, I had struggled and fought a battle within myself about whether to report the injustices that I had endured. I wanted to file a congressional, I wanted to file an equal opportunity (EO) complaint...I wanted justice for a wrong. I wanted to progress in my career, ...and yet I felt as though someone had stripped it from me. But then I remembered....*Lord, not my will, but yours be done. Even if I have to give it all away...then so be it.*

At some point, I decided that the greater gain would be to let the anger go. The greater gain was to forgive those who had hurt me, and my family. The greater gain would be to focus on what was important. So I chose not to fight the battle that way. Yet, while meditating, I began to put the trials together, weaving them to find a common thread. I remembered the experience with the promotion to Major when I first began to use the word to fight my battles. I applied the word and my faith and everything worked out for my good. Then I remembered the challenge in Kansas...an even greater challenge, but through intercessory prayer for others and by speaking and believing the word in faith, the Lord elevated and favored me yet again. So what was different now? I decided to let it go and focus on helping others. That was another shift!

I had been in Cocoa Beach for over one month...two months since the detection of the mass. Then one day out of the blue, my instructor told us a story about how she had just lost her best friend from cancer. Her friend was the type of Christian who had said that the Lord will work it out, and she refused to seek medical care. The friend believed she could sit in place and watch the Lord move her mountain/her cancer. The instructor, obviously sad, shook her head and said, "if only she had gone to the hospital." Quite naturally, my ears and everything in me stood at attention. Her words struck a chord in me. There was a churning in my stomach. I was innately familiar with this churning. Usually, when the Holy Spirit guides me, it is through this direct motioning in my gut. Maybe that's what many describe as a gut feeling. Nonetheless, I knew this was yet again, a warning signal and an instruction to move now.

As I think about the process of warning signals and divine instructions, I can't help but think about the fact that God loves me so much that he would send multiple signals....three at this point...the Apostle, Mr. George, and now my lovely instructor. God loves us so much, he will get a message through anyone he chooses. We just have to be open to listening. This method of divine communication also gave me encouragement because God obviously wanted me informed, he wanted me healed. That alone, even now, encourages me. If we can accept his instructions and guidance and accept his blessings and not let the devil take what is rightfully ours, then we can carry out what God has for us and others.

After hearing my teachers' story about her friend, my cell phone rang immediately afterwards. I went outside and took the call. It was Mr. George. In a sweet, respectable manner, Mr. George said "Ma'am, you were on my mind..have you gone to the doctor yet"? I sheepishly answered "no, Mr. George." Mr. George then politely, but firmly interrupted and said, "Major Buchanan, go now"! I immediately dropped everything and approached my instructor and said that I had to go to the hospital. I knew students should not miss class under any circumstances, so I had to get special approval to go to the doctor during class. I knew also that if I got a bad medical report, I would be disenrolled, and I would not be able to work as an advisor to the Commanding General. So, I prayed that the Lord would work everything out.

As for Mr. George, I would only speak to him one more time

that year before he went home to be with the Lord. His work was complete. I had been a part of his divine assignment. I thank the Lord for Mr. George..that soft spoken, Caucasian gentleman with the highest integrity and love of mankind. Through him, I experienced a true example of love for your neighbor. My friendship with him made everything in Kansas worth enduring. May he rest in peace.

The first appointment-

As I think about it all now, it seems everything happened so quickly. My life changed that day in September, 2008. My medical appointment was scheduled for the next morning, as the hospital fit me in without delay.

I started the process like many people according to the countless stories I have heard. This time, I was at the center of the story. I walked into the room knowing what the results would be, yet wanting to deny the signals that I had received. *Was this the transitionary trial I was to endure, but not yield to defeat? For if the diagnosis proved positive, was this the report that God said that would not harm me or take my life?* If it was, why had my mind abandoned that notion and think of death anyway?

The journey officially began: first I received a MRI scan at the military hospital, then I was referred out to get a needle biopsy (which I am not a fan of) to sample the breast tissue by a pathologist. As I met with the doctor who had read my MRI, I remember sitting with him in a small dark room. The doctor's accent was thick, and I could barely understand his words, but I clearly felt his fear and apprehension. We both were seated facing a triple-monitor X-ray screen. He sat on the left and then began pointing to the various dark spots on the screen which represented various angles and pictures of my right breast.

None of what I was hearing made any sense even as he said many things. Why didn't I understand him? Perhaps because what I wanted to know he wasn't saying. It seemed as though he was filibustering the inevitable. What I wanted to know was the truth. Tell me the facts. Let's get down to the facts. "Please confirm for me if I have this dreaded disease"? I asked. His face went pale in that darkened room. He answered me and said, "Ma'am, the dark spots on the report indicate malignancy." I caught his words finally and tuned into the word malignant. I replied, and asked again "what are you really saying doctor"? He shakingly paused, clearly averting the truth. I certainly was not postured for a sugarcoated roundabout answer. I felt my lioness rising, so I took a deep breath. "Sir," I said as softly and as patiently as I physically could express in an overly articulated staccato pace, "**please-tell-me, does malignant mean I have cancer"?**

He paused again. We were like two animals in the night staring at each other, each on guarded ground. He took a deep breath, and slowly said, "yes ma'am."

I stood up in a slow motion. My mind raced around and around. Did this man just tell me I had cancer? Then I thought about that mass. I thought about how it just appeared out of nowhere. I thought about my life and scanned through the years. What did I do Lord to have to endure this? How could a person physically fit get this disorder or was it because of a lifetime of stress on the job or with the family? What had happened here?- how is it that this little mass had come to invade my life? I even thought about the sin in my life, especially my past secret sins....was this punishment because of me?

In suspension of mind, something in me knew I had to leave this office. Though he was not my enemy, I felt an inclination to pour out the overflow of my emotions on him or someone. The room started to close in on me. I felt my breathing escalate. "How do you know it is cancer"? I emphatically questioned. "How do you just look at a picture and say, you have cancer? I cannot believe this! I just can't"!

So, if the doctor was hesitant in his discourse before, he certainly was hesitant now. The lioness in me had just stuck her head out. Oh boy. Ok, so I knew at this point, we were about to go down the road to Abilene. First, I put lioness Trece back in the cage, I composed myself and then asked. "Alright doctor, what's next? What do we need to do to confirm this diagnosis and to get this cancer out? What is it"?

The doctor hurried me through and said, call and make an appointment, and we will get back to you in a couple weeks and he hurried out the room. Quite naturally, I was devastated that someone would say-make an appointment we will get back with you in a couple weeks. My memory of this makes me want to share all of the ungodly names I uttered in my heart about those directions, so I will reserve them and repent again. At this point, I made my way into the hallway. Though mentally frail and exhausted, I leaned against the wall and looked at all the people pass by. I prayed....

Lord, give me strength, I need you now. My family is not here, I feel alone and afraid. Please guide me now. You said you would never leave me nor forsake me. Please help me Lord. Help me now!.

A stranger in uniform stopped and said, "Ma'am are you alright"? Although I was not alright, I was in uniform, so I had to maintain my composure. It is a military thing I suppose, or pride I suppose. Either way, I had to get myself together. My legs were weak, I literally felt like fainting, but my mind said,

"Stand up." At that point, I decided I would not call and make an appointment. I decided that I would get a plan that day. I prayed again, *Lord, extend your hand of favor and make a way.*

I walked what seemed to be ten feet, and to my right was a small booth with a male receptionist seated. The older white male slid his window open, though he was on the phone. I waited. When he got off the phone, he said, "Ma'am, may I help you?" I looked at him, weakened and with water-drenched eyes, although the tears weren't flowing. Softly I said, "Sir, I need to see a doctor, please." His reply was "have you made an appointment"? I was too tired to fight, so I took a long pause, and a deep breath before answering. I had prayed before, so I expected God to work for me. I couldn't do it. Then I asked very slowly with complete purpose with an unflinching gaze directly to his heart of hearts... "Sir, do you have a wife or a daughter"? He thought the question out of sync and strangely odd, but he softly answered and said, "yes, I do." As humbly and softly as I could, I then asked then, "what would you do if your wife or daughter was alone at the hospital and they received devastating news about their life? Would you want someone to help them"? He heard my cry for help. That day, the Lord worked through this angel stranger to make the call to get me some help. *I thank you Lord for the people, known and unknown and even the fearful ones in my life who got me where you wanted and needed me to be.*

Within minutes, I met my assigned primary care doctor while stationed at Patrick Airforce base for school (remember, I am an army girl on an Airforce base).

This African-American doctor was nice and comforting. He first wanted to take my blood pressure. We laughed because I remember saying, "there is no need to take my pressure, it is through the roof." We laughed through a not so funny moment.

The doctor got me organized, he helped put a plan together for me, to get a biopsy and helped with the entire administration of paperwork. He was another angel in disguise.

The day of the biopsy finally came. I had to travel in town for the procedure. The civilian clinic was full of patients, and it was chaotic that day, but I did finally manage to see the doctor who performed the needle biopsy. All I really remember was that I got my breast numbed, and I remember a very intimidating needle. The nurse inserted the needle, there were clipping sounds like cutting meat, and then the procedure was done. Though my breast was numb, I said to myself, oh my, how is this going to feel when the medicine wears off? It wasn't that bad though. There was some soreness but no real pain. Ironically, the weather that day was fierce. We were in the middle of a hurricane, and it was bad. In retrospect, that is probably why the clinic was in a chaotic state that day. Once I had completed the biopsy, I had to wait for the results. That wait was heart wrenching. Now after countless conversations with other people who have been through similar biopsies, there is little we can do to avoid the heart wrenching wait. People generally are scared, uncertain and they fear the future. My waiting period was longer than the norm. The hurricane had monsoon-like characteristics. It reminded me of a time in Korea where the storm waters were so high we were locked inside at elevated levels for over one week. This was the case in Cocoa Beach. The hurricane ripped through the community destroying buildings and houses throughout. Perhaps this was symbolic. I was in the eye of the storm yet again. There was destruction and death all around, but the Lord said *"Not so. You can't touch this one."* And though the storms beat against us at every turn, and the waters slid in from small open crevices, we were not consumed by that very present danger. We made it through and were not harmed.

The eye of the storm did not grip us...neither was cancer going to grip me. This is how I had to frame my mind.

"Not so, said the Lord! Not so"! Little by little, God was showing me physically, in real-time, what grace is. I realized then, I didn't really know what grace was. Every day was an opportunity to learn how He gives us what we need and how he gets us through life's challenges for his divine purpose. ***His Grace is Sufficient..***

The storm persisted for several days. The debris and damage was incredible. As a result, there was additional waiting for the biopsy results. Not only that, but I had to wait even longer because my doctor got out of dodge and went out of town.... can you blame him? The normal two to five day process was lengthened to two weeks, for the test results to come full circle back to me. The waiting, though nerve-wracking gave me time to bond with new friends at school, and it gave me focused time at school. That was important as I believed that I would be disenrolled immediately, once I received the results.

The day finally came. The clinic called and asked me to make an appointment to review the results. Within my core being, I already knew the results. Since this was the first time experiencing cancer, it wasn't clear in my mind just yet that God always prepares you for the way ahead. Through my life it has been one discovery point after another. The doctor walked in and sat with me. I remembered that I hadn't discussed this process with the family at large, but Harvey was on stand-by in Georgia. As the doctor confirmed that the walnut-sized mass in my lower right breast was in fact cancer, I remember being numb yet again. I remember my heart beat rang loudly at the center of my ears until that was all I could hear. Everything the doctor said to me after that was unclear, as I was in a far-off zone. I was no longer near where he was. I was somewhere, but not there. Should I cry? Should I panic? Should I lose my mind? Should I scream? I was numb. Finally, reason tapped me on the shoulder. "Sista, Sista? Are you there? It's time for you to listen. It's time for you to plant your feet and stand up. This is a new journey, now you must stand up, face it. You must walk in it."

I refocused and began clearing my mind . "Okay, doctor, can you tell me, why did I get this disorder"? The doctor then began saying words I knew I would have to later study. Estrogen positive, HER 2 neu, lymph nodes...what does all this mean? And so it was, the beginning of a long study on the biology of breast cancer in a woman. The doctor spoke about chemotherapy as the initial treatment along with surgery. He mentioned that the cancer was Stage 2, and that I was in a good position for treatment and for full remission, because I also had two enlarged axillary lymph nodes, but we had to work immediately to decrease the risk of the cancer spreading throughout my body.

I left the office that day and returned to school. I had completed the core classes and was in the intern mode of the course. The school administrator was a tough Sergeant Major with a ten-letter name. Though tough on the exterior, I prayed she would recognize that I was an excellent student and allow me do my internship at home. I wanted my certification. I prayed for favor, and the Lord granted it. The school had been impressed with my work ethic and passion for the cause and wanted me to serve as a leader in the field of discrimination law and prevention, so they allowed me to graduate two weeks early, predicated on completing my internship on the job. I was grateful, but I knew the way ahead would not be easy. Upon graduation, I was going to a rapid deployment division with over 28,000 service members. These were the movers and shakers in the field of war. More than likely there would be few women at my rank, few blacks, and no-one with cancer. Knowing this, I would not let cancer be the driving force as to why I could not complete my job. I needed to be physically and mentally ready to deploy with my team. I was not going to let cancer stop me!

With school completed, I said goodbye to my classmates. First, I had to personally thank my teacher for sharing her story with us, as it had motivated me to initiate care. I also found time to spend with my school mate, a Master Sergeant(MSG) who was himself a brain tumor survivor, a Republican and a Christian. I had to thank him because he had stayed with me during the hurricane, as I had waited for the results. Back then, his wife was also on the phone, as we three prayed for healing by faith. She encouraged me with their testimony, of how she had prayed for healing for her husband when everyone else had given up on him. You see several years earlier, her husband had a brain tumor and had been committed for life to an institution when he could no longer function appropriately in society. The military had placed him in a mental ward as the end had seemed near. To all around, it seemed as though it was impossible for him to live through it and regain normalcy. As God would have it, my Master Sergeant friend would be delivered out of this mental bondage and restored to duty with his wife's faith and prayers and through the Grace of God. I remember clearly my time with this particular family. The testimony of how God turned the situation around for this Sergeant would help me to stand throughout my treatment process.

I finally called my family to tell them the news. As expected, a high panic took place, and I knew that I could not operate with negative energy. People began to speak as if I were going to die. I told them, we all are going to die, but I am not dying from cancer. Not right now.

I shall not die but live and declare the works of the Lord...
Psalms 118:17 (NKJV)

It was clear to me, at this point that I had to guard my ears. I knew this battle was going to be an up-hill battle, but if I was going to have a fighting chance to win, I had to equip myself and to surround myself with the proper tools for life. For me, that was God's Word. I called my mother-in-law, Morristeen Buchanan at that point and Dr. Eve Taylor, a friend and prayer partner.

I asked my mother in law to write me one of her precious affirmation books, which she is gifted to write in the spirit. She doesn't know it, but I carry that book and read it like I read the bible, continually. The book is full of the Word that contains specific scriptures she has received from the Lord to address the needs of my life. I carry it and often I read it aloud. I speak aloud God's words, so that they may become life to me. I speak the word and I ask God... **to command his angels to watch over me and guide me as in Psalms 91:11 (NKJV)**. I had learned this principle during my faith walk while in the trial related to my promotion to Major. It was now time to use this principle again and use it like I had never used it before. My weaponry was not a gun, it was my mouth, my knowledge of God's word and my ability to speak the applicable words to my situation. There was no time for panic. I needed a plan of action in the spirit - a spiritual battle plan. I needed the proper people on my team. So I called on Jesus and his faithful prayer warriors. At this point, God provided me what I needed and who I needed. **His Grace is Sufficient....**

I left the school within 48-hours of my diagnosis. I spoke to the staff, my Commandant, and my entire class of over one hundred classmates as we all cried in saying farewell. I had to plant my feet and begin walking down a new path. I realized then that my new mission and my new voice would start with this experience---a journey of faith I would later discover, would be my calling.

Back at homestation: I had to notify my career managers in Washington, DC. I was concerned because I believed they would transfer me to non-deployable unit and tuck me away from the world in another position. I insisted that they leave me in this deployable position. This position was postured to deploy in one year, and they wanted to have a qualified person and war-ready person in place. I told my managers then, that I was fully qualified, and I would not let cancer hold me back...I asked that they give me a chance. At that moment, I remember praying, again, the Lord heard my heart and granted me favor.

The next year was the busiest year ever. Working for the General was no non-sense. My General held me to a high standard, and he empowered me. I served as one of his top five advisors and my goal was to do my job as unto the Lord. In other words, my job was to serve my Commander, the U.S. Army, and most importantly the people, and the soldiers with the highest integrity. Since my previous leaders had set it up that I would not see the next rank, I certainly didn't have anything to lose. I was determined to serve in my last job with everything that I had in me. This meant, I wasn't going to be concerned with political correctness, I was going to continue to serve with brutal honesty, humility and with excellence. I was glad that the career managers allowed me to complete this assignment. I worked feverishly during the first year with my new staff, the General and his staff as we all prepared to go to Iraq.

Medically, I started chemotherapy. I had three rounds, and I believed strongly that I needed to get off that particular type of chemo. Something wasn't right about that particular drug for me. The side effects were horrific. As I sat in my morning staff calls with the General and thirty other key leaders, I would often feel the sweat pouring down my face like someone had just poured a full bucket of water over my head. That was also the time where my hair began to fall out. My peers noticed. You could hear the unspoken conversations of my colleagues, and you could see people staring-even though they didn't look directly at me. I could hear their thoughts-even though they weren't outwardly speaking. Their non-verbal actions spoke volumes. Given the highly competitive nature of this group of professionals, you could pick the genuinely sincere and sympathetic souls out of the group. You could count them on one or two fingers—no more. Their thoughts were she is a weak link, she should not deploy with us. Only the strongest in body and in mind should go. After all, who needs a specialist on discrimination, sexual harassment (I had sexual assault certification too) and assault in a deployed setting anyway? Little did my peers know....their colleague would turn out to be one of their strongest assets. Who would be better to understand war than someone who has gone through a real life battle? I could certainly understand the plight of the political/ religious setting among the Sunni, Kurds and Shiites as a woman of faith who understands world religion; who understands mistreatment given my experiences with prejudice and discrimination throughout my professional life. I would have these conversations with leaders later during my deployment.

As the year closed, I had completed three rounds of chemo, a lumpectomy and a whole lot of naturopathic care. Many people including my doctors and family disagreed with my naturopathic care and my discontinuing the chemo agent which by the way is no longer used. I began to learn at this juncture, that dependence on prayer and listening to the Holy Spirit within me was going to have to be my center guide. The life, the industry and the business of cancer proved fierce. It was like being on an ever-moving treadmill that kept increasing in speed and going up-hill. You start at an elevated posture, and you begin by running. While running at an elevated posture, you have to listen to a recurring stereo of sounds of what you hope to be the truth and compare it to factual information. The information you draw from could be information you move on that can save you or kill you. On the treadmill of cancer, you have to be centered and possess precise focus. When one fears death, and that is married with misinformation and people with varying levels of faith, it certainly makes for a whirlwind of confusion. It creates a space where you can't make good decisions for yourself. For me, the Holy Spirit came to my rescue to teach, instruct and guide me.

So, when the day came and my surgeon uncle called and chastised me for my choices, I steamed with anger. Not because we are different people and make decisions differently, but it was, what he said and how he said it. My next statement is not intended to hurt the family. It is intended to sew all the unique occurrences together to understand how God works and to reveal how **his Grace is all we need**. My uncle firmly stated, "Why are you taking this approach? Why are you trying to preserve your body? Get both your breasts cut off, get your uterus removed, stop worrying about having a baby, plus you are too old to have a baby anyway"! These words obviously shocked me. I politely and respectfully had to reject every direction my uncle articulated.

Life point: Follow your own inner compass. For me that is the Holy Spirit, for **the Lord's Grace is Sufficient.**

Needless to say, I spoke to many, many people, and in their defense, most people really don't know or understand the inner makings of cancer and how to really get at its core, but God does. This is why it is so important to lean and trust only the Father because when you are in a situation with no clear solution, you should seek only God for direction, stand on His word, thank Him in advance for the unseen, and always give Him credit for the victory when you see the manifestations of his finished works. The best way to find the answers in a maze of societal and medical confusion is to seek the Lord for direction—the answers are out there and grace will get us through.

I worked every day, never missing a project or assignment because of the cancer. However, at some point, my physical ability to run drastically slowed down and for the first time in eighteen years, I could not run as fast as before (I used to run ten miles a day at one point and always scored top scores on my physical fitness). My peers of course, viewed this negatively, as a point of justifying why I should not be the one to deploy with them. This was a humbling space for me because I had never been in a position to come in dead last on anything. What used to be my strongest point in physical fitness, now became a dreaded difficult activity. It was humbling. Peers and coworkers treated me as though I was less than. At that point, I conceded to a small degree. I said, the running may have degraded in that I don't move as fast, but I will move. I will hold my head up; I will put one foot in front of the other, and I will run. Sometimes I wondered if the Lord allowed my athletic ability to subside, to humble me, and cause me to lean on him alone and not my innate abilities. For according to **Ecclesiastes 9:11 (NKJV):**

Again I saw under the sun that the race is not to the swift,
nor the battle to the strong, nor bread to the wise,
nor riches to men of understanding,
nor favor to the skillful;
but time and chance happen to all of them.

In other words, I just had to endure. I had often wondered if those peers could endure a similar situation? I remember overhearing my all male staff whispering one day. "They said, did you see that? She just bust out in a full sweat! Also, did you see that weird food she was eating? Man! And did you notice she had on a different wig today," as they collectively and secretively laughed. Now, let me say, I was very close to my staff and believed they meant me no harm, but they still were talking about me. In my own time, I was able to speak to them each about the process of going through cancer. As you know, when someone gets a disorder, it affects one's entire circle of influence. Within months, breast cancer invaded our unit. I was then able to literally speak to each of my male staff individually as each of their wives discovered an unusual lump on her breast and had to go through the grueling agony of a mammogram, biopsy and the dreaded waiting period. Unfortunately, one staff member went through the process with both his wife and then with his mother-who eventually succumbed to the disease. Each man came to me to get comfort as they didn't have a clue as to how to process their emotions, and they certainly did not know how to fathom their loved ones possibly being struck with a cancer. How would they survive? How would the household survive? I was glad to be there for them. My new job in life, my testimony was to be a blessing and to help others with this process...this was a new lesson and a new discovery point for me.

Daily, I had to give myself regular shots of the Word. Even with my strong faith, I believe it had to be worked, stretched and tested. To get through the given test, one must apply the Word to pass. And the application of the Word first means you must believe God and his inspired Word as true, then you must act out your trust in him by lining up your actions to match what you believe. This means if the Word has revealed a promise of healing, then your mouth should not be saying things like, "I'm sick and tired." This would counteract all the scriptures of healing spoken. Third, you must hope....knowing that it is done in the spirit realm before you see it in the flesh.

Some of my favorite scriptures are:

1) *I shall live and shall not die, and will declare the works of the Lord.* **(Psalms 118:17)**

2) *But He was wounded for our transgressions, He was bruised for our iniquities. The chastisement for our peace was upon Him, And by His stripes, we are healed.* **(Isaiah 53:5)**

3) *When he heard this, Jesus said, "This sickness will not end in death. No, it is for God's glory so that God's Son may be glorified through it.* **(John 11:4)**

4) *O LORD my God, I cried out to You, And You healed me.* **(Psalms 30:2)**

5) *Bless the LORD, O my soul; And all that is within me, bless His holy name!*
Bless the LORD, O my soul, And forget not all of His benefits:
Who forgives all your iniquities, Who heals all your diseases,
Who redeems your life from destruction, Who crowns you with loving-kindness and tender mercies. **(Psalms 103:1-4)**

6) He sent His word and healed them, And delivered them from their destruction. **(Psalms 107:20)**

7) Heal me, O LORD, and I shall be healed; Save me, and I shall be saved, For You are my praise. **(Jeremiah 17:14)**

8) For I will restore health to you And heal you of your wounds, says the LORD, 'Because they called you an outcast saying: This is Zion; No one seeks her. **(Jeremiah 30:17)**

9) Lord You are my Jehovah Rapha, God Who Heals. **(Exodus 15:26)**

10) Beloved, I pray that in all things thou may prosper and be in health, even as thy soul prospers. **(3John 1:2)**

11) A merry heart doeth good like a medicine. **(Proverbs 17:22)**

12) The thief cometh not, but for to steal, and to kill, and to destroy: I am come that they might have life, and that they might have it more abundantly. **(John 10:10)**

13) And He has said to me, "My grace is sufficient for you, for power is perfected in weakness." Most gladly, therefore, I will rather boast about my weaknesses, so that the power of Christ may dwell in me. **(2 Corinthians 12:9)**

14) Do not be anxious about anything, but in everything by prayer and supplication with thanksgiving, let your requests be made known to God. **(Philippians 4:6)**

15) Peace I leave with you; my peace I give you. I do not give to you as the world gives. Do not let your hearts be troubled and do not be afraid. **(John 14:27)**

*16)Do not let your hearts be troubled. You believe in God; believe also in me.***(John 14:1)**

17) I have told you these things, so that in me you may have peace. In this world you will have trouble. But take heart! I have overcome the world. **(John 16:33)**

18) Now faith is, the substance of things hoped for and the evidence of things not seen. **(Hebrews 11:1)**

19)....No calamity or harm will overtake me. **(Psalms 91:10)**

20) No ill befalls the righteous, but the wicked are filled with trouble. **(Proverbs 12:21)**

21) He will command his angels concerning you, to guard you carefully. **(Luke 4:10)**

22) ....Command your angels to lift me up so my foot does not hit up against a stone. **(Psalms 91:11, EJV)**

23)...No weapon formed against me shall prosper. **(Isaiah 54:17)**

24) So be strong and courageous! Do not be afraid and do not panic before them. For the Lord your God will personally go ahead of you. He will neither fail you, nor abandon you. **(Deuteronomy 31:6)**

At the one-year mark, my doctor gave me the green light to deploy. Medically, the tumor along with two lymph nodes and surrounding regions had been removed, and I had completed my chemotherapy regimen. There was no trace of cancer. Each month, I had taken a test called a CA27.29 marker test to see if there were traces of cancer. After receiving the all-clear sign, I then began my new normal routine. I was grateful that there were no traces of the disorder. I had to govern my mind and heart constantly to keep myself from thinking the worse. To help me with this, I constantly read the bible and my affirmation book of scriptures from my mother in law.

2009: Time to deploy....prep...mom sick....cruise lesson... deploy...holy ground...

The time was getting close to deploy. Sometimes, the thought of not going came into my mind. I could easily flip the script and provide a medical reason for not going, but something within me said, *do your duty*. The time has come for you to travel this road again, unfortunately without my family, dog, loved ones or friends. There was still something special about this journey. Briefing after briefing, I finally learned the area where our headquarters would be stationed. It was the area where Saddam Hussein had housed his Airforce, and it was a place known for having a soccer field where he had mass murdered many innocent people. The place we would occupy was also a place where Jesus, himself had walked the ground. From Tikrit northward towards Turkey, I was going to be on holy ground. I believed there was a reason I would go to that exact place. I knew in advance that while I would clearly be in a war zone, that this deployment would be with greater purpose. I knew the Lord would use this time for me to hear from him alone. This would only be the second time in my adult married life where I would have to travel away from home to receive of the Lord.

Sixty days prior to deployment, the entire division prepped to take thirty days of mandatory leave to be with family. This is referred to as block leave, during which I would be going on a cruise vacation with my family. Just prior to this period, I had to complete one more set of training and also break away to attend to my mother, who had become gravely ill. During this time, my team battle, who was my right hand senior enlisted advisor had to work hard to schedule the staff for this additional training as there had been multiple rollover accidents in the new tank we would be using. Congress had recently mandated this additional documented training for each deploying unit. As it happened, I had waves of family members coming in to visit, so I invited them to watch us go through a simulated rollover exercise at a facility with mounted vehicles. The experience was very physical and surprisingly a very spiritual exchange. To fully understand this story, I have to tie together the simulator story with one that deals with my mother.

At the simulator site...The instructing non-commissioned officer(NCO) firmly gave us directions as usual. There would be four of us in the mounted vehicle. I had to admit I was not in the mindset at that moment to be the vehicle commander. I sat in the front passenger seat, my battle sat in the back left and my training NCO sat in the back behind me. My operations sergeant was our driver. I remember the instructor and his team barking out the initial instructions. The main set of instructions were to refrain from grabbing this particular bar in the vehicle as it could cause direct harm. The instructors repeated these instructions several times," DO NOT GRAB THE BAR LOCATED HERE...it will cause you to get hurt." My heart was beating fast. I looked out at my happy family as they watched in excitement. I looked at each of my teammates in the vehicle, they were ready. I wasn't sure what to expect and didn't know if I was ready. The instructing NCO called out the signal on the intercom head set and asked if the commander was ready. First, I missed the cue, not realizing he was talking to me, this Adjutant General (AG) soldier. My infantry and artillery NCOs were looking at me. Quite frankly, they chuckled because they knew I was out of my AG zone, but this paper pusher had to get it together and lead. "Ok, we are ready," I said as confidently as I knew. The simulator began moving. It felt like being in a popcorn machine. We were tossed and thrown everywhere as the simulator rotated in full 360-degree turns. The experience was the first and last rollover I wanted to have. As the clock ticked forward, I thought to myself, I got it, I know this is serious but I want to get out. The timer finally stopped, and my staff and I were obviously all mixed up and seated upside down in full battle equipment. The next task was to get us all out before the next problem, a fire. If my team wasn't as close as we should've been then, we certainly became close. I knew we would each have to stick together during this journey. And we did. But as the four of us sat tangled, we had to move quickly to get out, as the evaluators had us on a time limit. Each one of us helped the other wiggle out of the confusing maze. One by one, the team got out. Of course, as the leader, I was the last to get out, and no, it wasn't out of generosity, it was because I was last. At some point the temperature in my body had risen as my anxiety of being stuck in a burning vehicle became more and more prevalent. I had to dig down and find a way to get out. I was stuck and my back was more than up against a wall. In the simulated space, I thought about all the soldiers who had really been in this space and who had not lived to tell about it. So for me, the simulation was real. I had to get out. I had to conquer the fear element that kept me bound. And while my team and family cheered me on from the outside, I once again had to plant my feet and survive this challenge. I didn't pray this time. I didn't think to pray, my butt was in a turned over vehicle about to explode and God needed me to act -to move out smartly. No time to pray, only time to act. I instinctively grabbed the forbidden bar the instructors had said not to grab. Of course, everything in me knew to follow their instructions but my body did the opposite. I grabbed the bar, I used it as a mechanism to hoist myself and to wiggle my way out. So while I wiggled, my thigh also hit the bar and I injured myself badly. Then of course, I saw the light. "Do Not Grab the Bar," yelled the instructing NCO, "Do not grab the frickin' bar ma'am"! But I had already done it. Grabbing the bar had obviously gone against the instructions. I got hurt that day, but there was a beautifully strange lesson that connected to my mother.

That same day, I got a call from the doctors saying that my mothers' condition had taken a turn for the worse and I needed to get home fast. My cruise was in one week, but I had to go home first. My mother had gone into the hospital for one thing, and ended up in surgery for another, which was then complicated by perforated intestines. Her health was spiraling downward. I stayed with my mom for a week until she got out of the danger zone. During that time, we got all her paperwork completed for her power of attorney, living will, bills, etc. It was a precarious time, because I did not want to leave her, but I had to take the mandatory vacation before I deployed. My mind raced, and I worried. I didn't want to go on the cruise, nor did I want to deploy leaving my mom. I had experienced this particular pain before, and I remembered that I had to give these matters over to God.

Reflecting back to the year 2005, five years after my stepdad, Major General Sherfield had died. Mom had become very ill after aggressively drowning her sorrows and her grief in the bottle... Her frail beautiful frame could only take so much abuse, and the years of alcohol consumption and its dreadful bitter fruit had become clear and present. Dad's death, due to the same abuse, had created a wide space of emptiness and raw emotion for each of us: my mother, brothers and stepsisters as well as our extended family. I remember that time clearly because I felt an overwhelming need to be there for my mother, but I couldn't. I needed to activate God's word. I needed to lay all my burdens on him. He would teach me during that period that **"his yoke is easy but his burdens were light... Matthew 11:30, (NKJV)"** *What he meant by this was, Shatrece, give me your burdens, take it off your neck and put it on mine. In this space, I do remember getting these instructions from the Lord. He had said, "walk around your* *mothers' home seven times....just like Joshua did. Bless her and pray for protection for her, and give this burden to me." That year in 2005, I had followed God's instructions, and God had saved her, protected and provided for her.*

And now, the year is 2009, one week before a mandatory vacation, and a few weeks before deploying. I'm back at her death bed. I'm back in a space of worry and seemingly attempting to carry the burden myself. I finally closed out my mothers' affairs, briefed the family and handed the baton over. This was very hard to do. I had to walk away from my mother to carry out my duty and a divine assignment. One week after leaving my mother, I can't honestly say I had released her care to the Lord. I worried constantly. Days afterwards, Harvey and I were on the cruise ship. I would not enjoy that vacation since there was so much guilt and worrying about my sick mother. I called incessantly to check on the doctor's every move. During one of those conversations, the doctors said her condition had gotten worse. My panic meter went through the roof. I knew calling wasn't going to change the situation, neither was my ranting and fussing, but I did it anyway. Finally, my cell phone went dead, and we were in the middle of the sea, with no land in clear site. My back was up against the wall. All I could do was call on the Lord. What a set up I thought. I could do nothing else. But for those who know anything about prayer, we know this is our primary weapon, but so often we treat it as the last option or the last resort, when it should be our first means of attack. Here again, the Lord was cultivating something in me, taking me to another level. I had to catch it because He was preparing me for something greater.

That night on the ship, I sat on the balcony with my pajamas on and prayed for what turned into hours from about eleven pm to six am. I prayed like Hannah throughout the night, praying for a miracle for my mom. As the sea waters whispered quietly, I looked into the full blackness of the ocean, and I spoke to God with a firmness of tone, tears streaming down my face. I spoke to Him about my mother, and how I needed him to watch over her and to keep her. I asked him to lift this burden off of me so I could go forward and to do his will. I asked him to give me peace and to give me a sign that he heard me and that he would honor my request. Out of my mouth, I boldly and firmly asked the Lord, "Do you hear me God? do you hear me"? I asked this, looking at the bright eye of the governing moon and listening to the waves of the pitch black sea. "Do you hear me Lord? If you hear me, I boldly asked, then make a whale jump out of the ocean or do something so I can see"? After making that request, I quickly laughed at myself and quickly recanted that statement. I thought, ok Lord, don't do that one, for if a whale jumped out the sea, I would truly have needed some diaper support.

As the night turned into day, I sat down in a chair and just worshipped the morning in. Upon raising my head out of worship, I saw the bright sun rise and change the darkness into glorious light. The sunrise was marvelous. The Lord then blessed me with three signs: first, a dove flew across my view in the middle of an open sea; second, the Lord revealed himself through a beautiful double rainbow; third, as I inadvertently looked down, I saw a black bruise on my thigh which seemed to just appear out of nowhere. The bruise took up most of my thigh and was in the shape of a whale. Inside that picture was another picture shaped like a whale. I could not believe my eyes, I had asked the Lord for a sign that I could trust him to carry my burdens and to work out the things that mattered the most and my Lord had sent me a dove, a double rainbow and he sent me a whale in the belly of a whale. I had asked the Lord to send me a whale as a sign and he was faithful. What an awesome God! He loves me so much, He got a message to me in the most peculiar manner. At this point, I gave the issue of my mother over to the Lord, finished the cruise enjoyingly, and later deployed to Iraq to begin this new journey. The Lord had cultivated a spirit of trust in me. This was the hardest part of my faith walk, the trusting that is.

So grabbing the simulator bar that day not only got me out of a dangerous situation, but the resultant bruise on my thigh (in the shape of a whale) would be the sign I would ask for later as I released my mother to Him. Wow! God knew I would ask for this sign even at the simulator and had worked it out before I even asked. This strengthened my belief - **His Grace is sufficient.** I would desperately need to draw from this lesson later in my life.

Chapter 2

The Second Time Around

I said all my farewells. I had a nice birthday party in September where my dad, Bobby, uncle Wilbert, aunt Emily, and so many friends came to visit. I appreciated that because my time away would be worrisome for the family. Many people didn't understand why I had to go. For me, it was my duty and my honor to go. But most importantly, I knew it was time that I needed with the Lord by myself, for it was during these difficult times alone where I received the most from the Lord. No worries of home, bills, wifely responsibilities....it was just me and God. I remember hugging Harvey, and I remember saying I love you. He kept me in his embrace. At that very moment, I remembered when I had to leave home for the first time to Korea. It seemed as if Harvey had gone into a space of denial and didn't believe that I was leaving. I clearly remembered him being more emotional than usual at the airport. I had to do an about face and walk away. I was a soldier and a wife, it was hard then, and it was evident, that this departure would be equally hard. It was finally time to get on the bus with my fellow soldiers. I sat at a window seat as the bus sat in the parking lot, parallel to the sidewalk, where family members gathered.

I looked out the window and almost broke. Harvey placed his hand on the exterior window pane where I sat looking out. He said as he cried out, "please don't go." My heart sank, and I cried silently, as the bus rolled from the Fort Stewart unit parking lot, on to the next destination. I had to plant my feet, take a deep breath, and walk out this journey, alone with my Father. Many people had taken this road to war and did not return home. I still had many questions, but overall I knew we had been well-prepared. I knew that the airbase we would occupy still had enemy activity, but not as much as years before. The threat was still active, but we had to go nonetheless, for the particular mission at hand. Traveling to Iraq was long and grueling. We endured long bus rides, long waiting periods in Savannah, Atlanta, and in German airports and finally in the Iraq reception area. Once in country, it took at least 3-4 days to transition into the war zone.

In Iraq, the operational tempo changed like a palpitating heart that skipped a beat. There seemed to be an interruption of time and space. One minute everything looked normal...people were going about life with concentrated focus. People were talking on phones and driving their cars, going to restaurants, just doing their own thing. Then we entered another zone, culturally distinct and definitely a war zone. Here, there was a concentrated effort within the group to be ever watchful and on guard. It was especially noticeable when we changed from a commercial plane to a war painted plane. The engines were open and loud. It was as if we were at the Indy 500 with all engines wrapped inside the back tail of that Boeing beauty. She roared fiercely.

The new mission had begun. The leading NCO hurled out the instructions for us to gather our bags and load from the back of the plane in full battle rattle. The equipment was heavy on my back, but my battle, MSG Smith, pushed me along. He never left my side. I remember before leaving Fort Stewart, this beautiful human being had told my husband that he would bring me back home safely. He had promised. I would later learn, this man was my assigned angel, though at first he truly worked my nerves as thoroughly as possible. We mounted that aircraft and everything was quiet, except for the sounds of the engine. With ruck sack dismounted in between our legs and weapons standing erect, we flew from the reception area into our new living space-Tikrit, Iraq, a place where Jesus himself had walked. I called it holy ground.

Once we arrived at our new home, so to speak, my team and I had little time to adjust before taking over the mission. The outgoing unit had already departed and hence there was no crossover time. I remember within the first week, the primary staff officers flew to Baghdad for an in brief by night flight. Thirty to forty primary leaders who would create the heart and pulse line of this battle, all tucked in the rear of a combat ready Boeing aircraft, with her war face painted and battle rattle fixed and ready to fight. There was an Asian-female trooper standing at the tail of the Boeing beauty. As the aircraft pressed upward in a parallel vertical manner, it was a seamless motion from ground to air. Our young trooper stood fearlessly in the back, she handled her business with weapon in hand guarding the rear, wide open to nature. I watched in awe. Our troops have done so many wonderfully brave things that the world has never witnessed, and so are unable to fully appreciate. We flew with purpose as I prayed for our safety. Iraqi country was beautiful in its natural form, but there were clear earthly bruises. In one moment you would see God's wonder of palm trees standing shoulder to shoulder for miles on the eye. In another view, you would see the dry scales of a war-torn earth.

The mission had to keep going, so upon our return we got set up quickly in our chus, which was a trailer without a bathroom or shower. I went without many luxuries that year in order to solely tune in to work and God. I opted to forego TV satellite services for a year, although I had a DVD player. There was no bathroom, as was the case with most soldiers. Instead, we walked to a community commode and shower located about 500-feet from our living area. My team and I would have to either walk, cycle, run or drive 1.5-miles from our workplace in order to get to the headquarters to see the boss. We spent that year working discrimination , sexual harassment and sexual assault cases. Inasmuch as it would seem that there was no need for this service in a deployed setting, think again, there was, and it started for us from day one.

My chu was located near the Generals' headquarters. I needed to be near his operation for morning and evening briefs, while my office was in a former Iraqi Generals' space. We were set apart from most of my peers because of the sensitive work we did. We did not have bunkers surrounding our space initially, which left us vulnerable to daily attacks because we were next to a refuel point. The enemy knew this and frequently aimed at that direction to destroy our capabilities. After three to four months, that issue was solved.

We sat in the center of the country, Baghdad was south of us and Turkey was to our north. We had units throughout and around the disputed international borders(DIBS) which was the heart of the problem within the country. In layman's terms, the Iraqi people were culturally, religiously and politically in harsh divide. Politics, religion and culture were innately apart of each other and connected, as in a marriage. Our democratic process was in stark contrast to the sovereign order of the land. But a divorce of the old wine skin and new wine skin was imminent. At the core of this split was the issue of the Iraqis' most precious resource, oil. I remember the picture of this holy place as if it were yesterday. I remember seeing this precious resource seep up and out of the desert, like dried blood stuck to a maze of arteries cracked open and bruised. I would never forget that sight of the oil oozing from the center of the earth. Black veins I would often call it, black veins. Why had the Lord allowed my eyes to see this?

Interestingly, I also helped get the local church up and running, in addition to the many tasks that were involved in the setup of our chus, headquarters and the professional field.

My role there would begin as the de facto Pastor, and later I would become the official Pastor. My professional battles, MSG Robert Smith and MSG Rainey Young would also be my battles in the church as well. I am forever thankful for these two men of God.

Throughout the first half of the year, my health was in tip top shape. I ran or walked daily, and I participated in organized sports like basketball and tennis. I even joined a weight lifting competition in that year. I kept my hair short but decided to texturize it every several months. I refused to look too rough even in a warzone. I even wore my lipstick, Yes, I did. This was one luxury I did keep. For whatever happened there, I would go through it, the way the mothers in my family had trained me... no plaits in the hair, dressed decently from the underclothes up with hair and makeup intact. Since the temperature there was God-forsaken fierce, my body stayed in a constant state of thermal heat burning mode.

During the first six months, my immediate staff heavily focused on consulate resolutions: counseling and mediation as well within the division. The civilians and contractors did not have the local support they needed to take care of interpersonal problems, or conflicts within their work place. In general, being in a deployed setting usually amplifies relationships either for better or for worse. You get closer or you don't. The high operational tempo contributes to the aforementioned. During this space and time, my team and I also got close to the foreign nationals, in particular those from Sri Lanka and Uganda. In forming the church, our new allies would flock to the church as well. We formed relationships that we enjoy even today. I was continually blessed by my son in the Lord - Joel and my pastor friend Peter from Sri Lanka. I thank God for them both. Joel, my son, had light brown skin and jet black hair. He was at the time 18 years old and had left his country, his family, his twin brother, his then girlfriend and church to serve time in Iraq as a cook. In his spare time he worshiped through music. In his home town, the young males in his family were trained from birth to age 16 years to first serve as praise and worship leaders. He truly blessed me as he sang to me everywhere. Joel, would often tell me he loved me. I loved him too. I still do. I would often ask the Lord what he wanted me to do with my new formed relationships.

Peter was also a Pastor, and my friend. He led the flock of international workers, a male camp from Sri Lanka, India and other countries. They would often get on me for calling Sri Lanka, India and India, Sri Lanka. Peter was also the leader of the dining facility, which was the main gathering place for the soldiers and contractors three times a day. Dining facility operations are a huge deal at war. It was the only time in the day where we as a unit could stop and come together away from battle operations to eat. Food was a big deal. We ate well, food was plentiful. The workers came from all over the world as the U.S. military paid so much better than if they had stayed in their own countries. Yet these wages were little to nothing per month by our American standard. It was equivalent to one third our minimum wage. Peter had worked for five years away from his family in total sacrifice to support his wife, two daughters, mother, father as well as his brothers. His entire family led a church in the main city outside his small village. He and his family were Christians, but their countrymen either did not believe in God or were Buddhists. God put us together, for a reason initially unknown to me.

My battle or partner, MSG Smith, and I went everywhere together, and he and I ate late most evenings. While in Iraq, Peter and I would sometimes speak at the end of the dining facility hours only for a moment since he was at work. As Peter and I talked, my battle would either catch up on the news or make his rounds talking to soldiers. He and I made perfect partners. It had taken time, but we grew into it, and I am grateful. Peter and I spoke about the Lord and we spoke about the needs of the people on our base. We shared as Pastors do. While Peter often wanted me to come to the male camp and speak to his countrymen, I would always send in some of my other male ministers. There were however opportunities for Peter to join us at our church. In the church, we had about seven ministers on staff, a choir, and a bible study core. With the oversight of the division chaplain, we were able to have an active congregation for the year of over 70-100 members. The Lord really worked on us all. We learned from the ground up. We dealt with everything as it occurred...constant study of the word, teaching, preaching, sharing of challenges, counseling, comforting, constant prayer and intercession, outreach in the community, training of leaders, baptisms, etc. I was honored to have had that experience.

In addition to the countless discrimination cases processed, I remember we also had the unique privilege to host multiple cultural sensitivity training events. One particular event highlighted Martin Luther Kings' Noble Peace Prize speech. We invited the President of one of the top universities and his leaders. Our job was to teach about peace to the teachers who would bend the perspectives of the upcoming generation of youth. I remember the leaders saying they had never heard of this speech about peace.

Throughout that year, there were countless stories where we felt as if our service truly counted. My General took pride in the relationship we forged with the Ugandans. I remember the first time I spoke in front of a crowd of 300 Ugandans.. They each sat with immense pride because they had never seen a black female at that rank. They were proud, and so was I. They probably thought in their heart of hearts that I was a Ugandan until I opened my mouth. I then heard a loud and thunderous laugh. The vibrations of my clearly American voice quickly sealed their curiosity. This sister was an American, not Ugandan. We enjoy this story even today. I did not know the complete picture of what the future would hold. Why was the Lord allowing me to speak to this group of people? Why was this relationship so important? That speech started a special bond between my office and the Ugandans. Although they were away from their land, they too, needed their rights and voices heard--better pay, fair housing, ability to work in a hassle-free environment, free of discrimination and sexual advancements. They also needed a place to worship in the way they believed. My relationship as mediator for the Ugandans paid many dividends for our units' protection, as they were solely responsible for providing security, in concert with our troops for the space we occupied. As a result, every Ugandan affectionately called me mom.

I had worked hard for my physical fitness test in the first few months in Iraq. I passed it with high scores. I had watched my diet, and fasted often for spiritual cleansing, for clarity, and to keep my flesh under subjection, all things considered. After the physical fitness test, which occurred around April, I remember slacking off a bit with my eating and exercise discipline. While

I kept a strict watch on the products I put on my skin, I do remember splurging after long periods of disciplined eating. I remember the sweet cakes in particular.

At some point finally, it was time to go home for R&R. Just prior to leaving, I remember the medic telling me I had to take the next anthrax vaccine. I had adamantly protested taking this shot for many years and gotten around it somehow, but at that moment I was in the hot seat. I couldn't avoid the shot any longer, as everyone in theatre had to take that shot. I remember clearly that month, May of 2010. I remember getting the shot in my right arm, which I should not have allowed, since my lymph nodes were removed from that particular arm.

I finally made it home. My R&R time away of fifteen days would go by quickly. I had work to do while at home. I had to get my taxes done, and get medically checked by taking a mammogram. My breast exam was scheduled at the nearby military post. I was accustomed to seeing civilian specialists and wasn't really accustomed to dealing with military hospitals. Nonetheless, I would remember that test day.

The technician said, "place your breast, right here and you will feel some pressure." The test caused me immense pain! I had had mammograms before, but this one was bad. My breast had been squeezed so hard, it would hurt for months afterwards. I began to get a feeling that something was wrong. My fifteen days ended, and I returned to Tikrit, Iraq. Upon returning, my breasts still hurt. My battle was next for leave, so we had to work with an abbreviated team. Once everyone got back, we would settle back into the 16-hour work days, 7-days a week schedule.

One day during the late evening dinner shift, Peter approached me with intense worry and asked to meet with me after the dining hall was empty. My battle, never leaving my side understood I needed to talk to Peter, so he sat quietly and waited for me. Little did I know MSG Smith heard our entire conversation, one I thought was private. In any event, Peter asked for prayer. We prayed. We prayed because his wife had just been diagnosed with an aggressive cancer. In Sri Lanka, medical care and insurance is not the same as in the U.S., so Peter would have had to immediately return home and absorb the major cost. We both were sad for many reasons. This dire situation would cut our relationship short. What I loved about our relationship was that while there were language barriers, our heartbeat was unified in leadership, and in our ministry. Peter was scheduled to depart in a matter of days. I needed to seek guidance with the Lord as to how I could be of service. In my quiet time, the Lord instructed me to plant a financial seed into the life of Peter and his family, by giving a designated amount monthly for four months. This money would cover the initial medical care for his wife, it would pay for his children's school for one year and it would serve as seed money for Peter to purchase supplies to open a business to sustain himself and his family after that first year. After receiving from the Lord, I called my husband to get into agreement. At first my husband had many questions, but he finally conceded by saying, "if the Lord said do it, then so be it."

I would thank God for this later.**Give, and it will be given to you; good measure, pressed down, and shaken together, and running over, shall men give into your bosom. For with the same measure that you use it, it shall be measured back to you... Luke 6:38 (NKJV)**

Peter and I met three more times before we said our goodbyes. In our first meeting, I informed him we would seed into his family.

He cried with thanks. Our second meeting was about business. We exchanged bank information, went over the business plan specifically and we went over the monthly instructions that the Lord had given me. I handed off four checks in blind faith. Peter accepted. He followed the instructions, and he did not waiver. He was and is a trustworthy man of God. We both followed what the Lord said. Our last meeting consisted of saying goodbyes to the countrymen.

> **Life point:** When God gives divine specific instructions, follow them. Do it immediately. Don't question. Don't waver. Do it in faith. The instructions you follow, could be the very thing that saves your life or brings you life later.

As the months rolled by, we all continued to work tirelessly, all looking forward to the time when we could finally go home. The church was thriving at this point. Each of the ministers under my charge were in a good rhythm and all of the auxiliaries were flowing well. Faithful members attended and the Word was preached. At some point, I noticed we began to get a lot of prayer requests for sick family members. Many members talked about family at home who suffered from cancer. I certainly could identify with that need. As the talk of healing became a predominant point of prayer and need, I began to wonder about myself.

In the months after returning back into theater from June to September, my breasts still hurt. I did not exercise as much because I had passed my physical fitness test, and was a little relaxed mentally and relieved of the pressure to condition and make weight, so I took a break. I oddly remember a particular night when I was in my room alone and bored. I picked up a DVD without looking at the cover and popped it in. This was totally odd because we worked most of the time. Daily, there was only time to work, eat a quick bite and sleep for a few hours. The movie was about a doctor in California who had spent 20 years trying to get a drug called herceptin approved. Herceptin is a targeted hormone drug used today for women with breast cancer. At the time, I thought it strange that I would arbitrarily pick this movie out of the mammoth stack of DVD's in my chu.

What were the odds? Was this a sign? Was I going to go through cancer again? Why were there so many testimonies and prayer requests about cancer in the church? I asked God all these questions privately.

I asked these questions because there was a secret I carried that I had not told anyone. After taking the anthrax vaccine and my last mammogram, my right breast had begun to swell, little by little from May to July. By the end of September, the swelling had progressed, but I still did not want to believe that there was a problem brewing. The first week of October came, and while we were supposed to go home, we received orders to stay thirty days longer. The swelling was now more than noticeable. Whatever was going on, it was no joke, and I needed to take action. My breast was abnormally swollen and hot. I believed there was an aggressive tumor inside and it was hot, angry and ready to take over. In the interim, I had to prepare. That night, I waited for the staff to go home. My battle and I always left together, so he was in his office, and I in mine. Battles' wife had just sent him a beautiful praise and worship CD, so I heard him in there playing it loudly. I approached. I asked him if we could talk, and he knew something was serious. I sat at his desk. I told him that I believed that the cancer had returned. He asked me a few questions, he comforted me and then began to minister to my spirit. He told me to trust God with all my might. He then said let us praise Him now. We turned up the worship music in our workplace, in the middle of the night and we worshipped and we both cried. I thank God for my battle. Afterwards, I knew I could not cry for too long. I knew it was time for me to go home. I would use the next 72-hours to go to the doctor, quickly close out my office and the affairs of the church. I wrote my last sermon. I wrote letters to my leaders in the church and left instructions on maintaining the call of discipleship and stewardship. I also wrote a letter to the congregation.

Prior to my last week in country, I do recall telling the ministers of my situation. They gathered around and all of them prayed over my life. There were at least seven leaders. They prayed, and I remember Minister Bridgett, saying in her prayer, "not so, says the Lord"! At this point, there was a quickening in my spirit. Here were the exact words spoken over my life from my apostle from the year, 2008. Now, it was two years later, and the Lord was saying the same words to remind me that he was not going to leave me and that the enemy was not going to win my life. *"Not so, says the Lord"!* I believed this with all my heart. Those few words, gave me enough courage to face the future.

After meeting with the ministers, I passed on their instructions and handed the baton to Minister Bridgett. I also notified my General and told him that I believed the cancer had returned. He told me to go on ahead and be well since I would not be able to complete the last week with the team.

My battle wanted to go also, but I refused to let him alter his schedule. The flight plans were very stringent and any change in schedule could impact family reconciliations and plans on the returning end. Battle had family obligations and I was not going to have him interrupt that under any circumstance. Because I insisted on going alone, he employed the assistance of other non-commissioned officer(NCOs) to care for me as I traveled back to the U.S. That's what battles do, and he had promised Harvey. And so it was, yet another journey to travel. I had to plant my feet and face this next hurdle in my faith. Along the way, I would continually lean on the fact that I knew that **God's Grace is Sufficient**. He provides everything when needed. I had made it through a year deployment on holy ground. My mission there was complete. We had faithfully served the people and fed them with the Word. We had met foreigners throughout our travels and formed lasting relationships. There was more to come.

Upon returning to the U.S., my first stop after meeting my husband was straight to the doctor. I would see my previous surgeon. She would take one look at the grapefruit size tumor that now consumed my right chest, and immediately say your cancer has returned. It appeared to be a different type, and very aggressive. I asked the doctor to confirm it through administering a biopsy. She numbed the breast and pressed deeply inside the middle of the tumor with a needle. The procedure was quick and relatively painless. Once she sent in the sample to the pathologist, reports confirmed my second bout with cancer, two years after my initial diagnosis. The same feelings came tumbling back as with the first notification. Although I didn't fall against the wall or lose it, much was the same. I thought, *What is going on with my body? What triggered the acceleration of this tumor? Why was it growing so fast and so big? What could be done immediately to get it under control?*

The shock effect felt the same as if someone had called you and told you someone you loved dearly had died. The effect, and the feeling were synonymous. Although death danced and dangled and taunted me, I still did not yield to the notion because I felt there was time to fight and to fight hard. I chose not to panic. After all, the Lord has always had my back. He had been preparing me throughout. "*Not so, said the Lord*"...is what I remembered. It would be the phrase that had kept me and would keep me around for a long while. The doctors on the other hand were very concerned. I wasn't going to succumb to panic this time. I had to remember what God had told me. So I focused on that instead - "*I will live and not die.*" I calmly asked the doctor, "what do we do now concerning the way ahead"? She threw in a sneak punch I felt, by suggesting that I had caused this on myself by not completing the chemo regimen. First of all, I thought to myself -chemo does not cure cancer. And there have been many who have died from complications related to chemotherapy. I disregarded her sneak punch and asked again, "what is the way ahead doctor"? She told me, with a quivering, nervous lip, that she could not do surgery because the tumor was too big. I was totally taken aback. "Are you refusing to do surgery, I asked?" She pretty much said, "Yes. You must get the tumor shrunk to a smaller size before I can do anything." The doctor knew my position on taking chemotherapy. I knew then, I had to go within myself again to figure out prayerfully and intuitively what I needed to do next. The doctor could not make that decision for me, nor could anyone else. I had to go within to find the best answer for my life. The way ahead would be a road of tough choices.

I went away that day not knowing which way to go. In the previous two years, the conventional medical system seemed still stuck on one treatment protocol to solve this disorder. To take chemo or not. To cut or to not cut or to burn by radiation or not?

Those were seemingly the only options. I wasn't satisfied with those options. I initially felt lost and distraught, but the Lord had so filled me with himself, I would not stay depressed and downtrodden. I think more than anything else, he put a natural trigger in me to fight and to refuse the status quo, and to always question intensely what appeared to be foolishness and craziness. He did not make me a conformist, I realized. Perhaps I was the agitator on causes that seemed to take people down the road to Abilene. For me, I had to respond and act. But within myself, I knew the status quo was not the best fit for me.

Within a span of days, the Lord brought to my memory a clinic in Ashland Oregon, named the Mederi Centre for natural healing and its research foundation. I had learned about Mederi, as I visited a Brighter day, a local health food store and gem in the heart of Savannah, Georgia, located on Bull Street. Brighter day proved to be my physical haven here on earth. I believe they were singularly responsible for my progress and healthy lifestyle today. As I navigated through the maze of medical support, I decided I would get a second opinion and arranged for a transfer of my treatment to Florida. The Mayo clinic would now provide my care. The oncologist and surgeons in Savannah had done their best, but I wanted another perspective, and I wanted a place where all the care was in the same facility. While beating the pavement weekly going from Georgia to Florida, the miles and the stress mounted. The up-tempo in returning from war was high. It was like returning to your house after a year of being away. The grass needed to be cut, maintenance around the house had to be addressed, administrative work had to be conducted, and then I had to get to know the people I once was close with...sort of like being strangers uniting for the first time. There was a time adjustment initially and there certainly was a climate adjustment. It seemed my body was still in some sort of heated thermal mode.

At work as well, the entire division was chaotic back in Georgia. There were rear detachment people merged with the permanent party personnel, so the work spaces were crowded. Each department had the same activity. We had to unload our equipment from the shipment containers and get them back inside our offices. We had to receive our deployable vehicles and unit items and reconcile with the company. So the company commanders had daily requirements from the battalion commander and the commanding General needed us also. This was the unique feature in working directly for a General, somebody still had to run the battalion and my wonderful sister, Colonel Nora Marcos, executed operations seamlessly. With all this movement, I still fit in time to get to back and forth to Florida.

The doctors at the Mayo Clinic were professional and the services were more convenient. I was able to get all the tests done in one setting. The team confirmed the original findings and their discourse was the same as in Savannah, GA. The lead oncologist, in my view was text book and it was apparent he did not have a warm bedside manner. I knew this relationship would have a defined start and end point. The surgeon was young and hugely arrogant. It seemed he preferred to be right in knowing that the only course of action would be to take chemo for a while to shrink the huge mass and then to remove the entire right breast. I was opposed to the removal of my breast. I was completely uneasy with the idea, to say the least, so I waited with a feeling like I was in a box that was shrinking towards the center, second by the second. Time passed, and Harvey and I traveled to Florida faithfully. Eventually, I did begin taking the recommended chemo treatments from the Abraxene line after a second opinion with my trusted stakeholders from the Mederi Centre for natural healing.

At this time in my life and at this point in dealing with this tumor, I was not fully active with Mederi. The staff at Mederi are forward thinkers and they are the soldiers on the frontline binding our wounds and preparing us to fight and live forward. I was introduced to Mederi through the owner at Brighter day who would be another stranger angel sent to me on this road I sojourned. The owner and I just ran into each other one day. We began to talk about my situation and he stopped cold in his steps and said let me share something with you. He then saved and printed at least ten free copies of Mederi - Donald Yance's personal lectures for me on the spot. He gave them to me out of the kindness from his heart. **God's Grace is Sufficient.** He always provides you with what you need, right on time. Mederi was instrumental in providing me with good research explanations on the latest cancer developments. They were and still are one of leading clinics that understands how to treat cancer from a holistic stand point. Mederi does everything to not harm the whole patient- body, mind and soul. They are able to encourage the use of traditional cancer treatments including chemotherapy with a strict blend of holistic practices that help protect a person from the potential harmful effects of chemo.

I began to listen to those CDs, relentlessly. The information I received, opened up my soul. I often would shout in praise because I could not believe how God is so good, that he would allow me to have and hear information that no main stream hospital or clinic had thus far articulated. So I began to question this. Why is it that when we are sick from cancer, why don't our nations' best minds not provide this information that God had dropped in my lap for free? Is it that somewhere along the way our system got blind sided with the lure of money and greed? I knew then that this would be an uphill road, against institutional ills and better yet spiritual strongholds of drug dependency, greed and control. This would certainly be something God had to battle. And I would simply follow his lead.

As the days moved along, the tumor began to shrink with chemotherapy. I endured the side effects of hair loss, bloody noses, black toe nails, black stool in some cases, and the jump starting of even more hot flashes. Overall, while this may sound overwhelming, under no circumstance did I suffer during this period. I did not miss a day of work. I was in no major pain. God kept me. He preserved me in every manner.

Driving to Mayo...

I remember my heart racing this day. I had consumed Mederi's CDs, and it seemed I was learning something new daily. That day, Donnie had spoken about large tumors and what should be done for control. What I remembered is that while getting a mastectomy was inhumane, in some cases a decision for a mastectomy had to be made in the case of really huge tumors. I was in that category. I could not fathom someone cutting my breast off. My breast wasn't small. It carried 'a good chunk of change' I would say. It just didn't seem like the natural order of things. But that day, I had heard that there were many thoughts about penetrating the breast area with a contained tumor. To cut into the breast could make the cancer spread was one train of thought. Another thought, keep the tumor contained and do everything to shrink it....but keep it contained. Do not penetrate. So in this case, I had heard two train of thoughts. Which should I do? What I did know at the time, was that the tumor was not the norm. I knew the doctors were not going to budge. They were sticking to their guns and would stick together by hook or crook. I tried to resist the feeling of being alone. What do I do now? While it had shrunk from the original size, it was still a force to contend with. Every instinct in my body and soul knew deep down inside what I needed to do, but the comments of others were confusing. I settled it with God that day. The Lord gave me peace with this decision. I knew with certainty, I wanted that stinking tumor gone, and I wanted it out of my body. At that point, I had lived everyday with the tumor in my body now for ten months... It seemed like my back was up against a wall again, but God said, *"not so, you shall not die."*

Help me Lord. Guide me. Give me peace, I prayed.

And then I got the peace and the courage to proceed with my decision. I decided to have the tumor removed. I had fought with the surgeon for a couple weeks. But I had to relent. I realize I have a tendency not to get along well in situations in which doctors are arrogant and dictatorial Also, many of the doctors I have dealt with were culturally insensitive with respect to my spiritual beliefs in God. I quickly rebounded and repeatedly had to ask these doctors to respect the spiritual aspects of health. At the end of the day, God made everything. He made the doctor. He made the doctor's mind to think. He made the plants and the earth which man has appropriated well and not so well. He made healing. And healing is an option for all. I believe that doctors who don't know or respect that position, should at least respect the patients' belief system. Throughout this process, I have slowly come to the realization, that this experience has affected me, but it is not entirely about me or my life. It is all about God getting the glory, and to allow someone the opportunity to be saved and receive the free gift of Jesus Christ.

I also learned then, that I can't fire every doctor who just doesn't know or understand the mind-body-soul connection, I had to weather that storm also. At the end of the day, I am a living testimony, a walking disciple. The doctors may not want to hear the Word in the work place, but my life, kindness and continued faith will continue to shine as the example, better than any argument or break in relationship. Jesus will be glorified. I just needed to get in the room and let God do what he does best. He heals each of us at the very place we need healing...whether that be cancer or arrogance.

Life point: Peace was my guiding point at this moment. How does one truly trust God and walk in faith in situations like this? The doctors gave me one option which they believed gave me the best chance for living. But when dealing with God, my life lesson was that I should trust God in the midst of uncertainty. God does not belong in a limiting box. So I believe that I should work with what I have and believe God to reveal more in his perfect timing. I needed to rest in my decision, and I knew with or without a mastectomy, God can fix every situation. With a breast or without it, I believe I am healed. I believe one must make a decision, that gives you peace within. Afterwards, we should live like you will live for sixty more years in your mind, heart and soul. And if for some reason, your body expires to the pounding of this disease, because we are all going to pass away one day, you still receive your healing in faith. This may confuse some, but the journey of walking through any type of health disorder can be taxing on your mind and soul. It does not have to be. Hold on to what God says and rest in it, no matter what happens. The devil can't steal your joy in the Lord. He can't steal your confidence in the Lord. Our bodies will pass away, but you have direct control of your mind and your spiritual standing.

These things I have spoken to you that in Me you may have peace. In the world you will have tribulation; but be of good cheer, I have overcome the world.

John 16:33, NKJV

All that being said, my surgery was scheduled for October, 2011. I was having a total mastectomy, they were taking the whole right breast including the areola. I had to plant my feet, take a deep breath. I had made the decision, and I had to rest in God now. I finally followed through with what the doctors had recommended. The surgery was to be followed by a reconstruction with a South African surgeon, currently at Mayo. I actually liked this doctor, he was reportedly an outstanding breast reconstruction surgeon. Reconstruction would require travel back and forth to Florida for some time to get the expanders filled. Within two months of my initial surgery, I developed serious respiratory complications that I had not foreseen. As a result, I asked the doctor to remove the expanders. The month was now December, 2011. The second surgery was performed late at night, and the South African doctor, accommodated me graciously. I believe this gentleman doctor was genuine, and I believed that he truly cared for me along with his other patients. His staff also reflected his professionalism and care. In the coming months, there would be another shift in the tide.

Chapter 3

The Third Time Around

Three months had passed since my surgery, and it seemed as though my wounds were healing okay. At least it seemed that way on the surface. Militarily, I was finally in sight of retiring honorably from service after 24 years. I had been on leave with pay since October, but my leave would end on February 1st, 2012. I felt a need to insure I properly transitioned my medical care so that there would be no interruption of service. I also had to take care of my life insurances. I had always had good medical benefits during my military service, and I needed to keep the same. As I shopped around, I was repeatedly told that I was uninsurable; no one would insure me because of the cancer. I was being medically discriminated against because of this disorder.

I also began to notice a swelling on my right chest at the previous surgical site. I needed to report it to my doctor and new oncology team. Upon retiring, I had to change the entire medical team, from February to April, 2012. I would struggle to seal a new team of providers and oncologists during that time. In the meantime, a new type of cancer would sprout out of my right chest wall. It was evidently clear that a mastectomy did not always cure breast cancer and certainly did not always prevent a person from getting another breast cancer recurrence. It was also clear to me that chemotherapy does not cure cancer. Chemo seems to cut the cancer at the top of the root. But ladies and gentlemen, the root still lingers and its fruit -the cancer was evident once again.

Next, I had to find a new primary care provider. I shopped around and selected a local clinic in South Georgia. A couple weeks after checking in, I received a letter from the clinic saying they could not provide medical care for me. "What? I didn't understand." The lioness in me surfaced. I wanted to roar, but I had to focus, fix my eyes and my ears on what was really happening. A nurse practitioner who was quick at the draw had made a bad decision for her doctor boss; she had disenrolled me because she believed I would prove to be a financial burden on the establishment. A huge injustice had occurred and something had to be done. I filed a formal complaint through the insurance company and allowed them to investigate. While I did not get the results I sought, at least the incident was recorded and some light was shed on the issue. The delay in care was significant, as the new tumor again grew, hotter and hotter, day by day.

During this medical malfeasance debacle with the local medical provider, I also had to find a local oncologist. I had finally selected a particular oncologist in the Savannah area, who knew my previous doctor and had shared notes. They were all on one accord and initially agreed to play ball. Quite naturally, they seemed to blame me for my woes. But first things first. There was a real and presently hot and angry tumor rising and spreading again. This time I could see first-hand how the tumor grew since it grew on my post-mastectomy chest wall. It was amazing yet utterly scary to watch this. Never in my life would I have imagined or wanted anyone to see the sight of a dozen tumors growing at record pace in front of one's eyes. Open tumors for my regular review.

Seeing the accelerated growth of the tumors was also hard for my husband. He would often appear glassy-eyed, as he privately struggled to understand what was going on. It was clear to him that there now was a foreign force in my body that he could see growing from the inside out, and that surely terrified him. It would take God to help him process this. And if that wasn't bad enough, his father was diagnosed with metastatic colon cancer - Stage 4 cancer and was going through his own process, though a little differently than I. He had chosen a highly aggressive regimen of chemo with radiation and was struggling. The excessive medication eventually led to liver failure because of toxic overload.

Life point: Protect the liver at all cost and never let the doctors over medicate. Small dosing is the key. Repeat... small dosages is the key and detox continually through holistic supplements, water therapy, a strict diet using red, yellow, orange seasonings in the turmeric-curcumin family. Do this. Do not get confused by doctors who say not to mix supplements with your treatment. Do what you must to live. I recommend you also call the Mederi Centre for natural healing in Ashland, Oregon and they will put a personal plan together to help you live. These people were my direct angels sent from heaven to keep me alive.

My sense of time and urgency was again on high alert. The tumors were growing on my right chest wall....they looked like expanded boils, some red, some jet white but all were bleeding. The situation was incredibly profound and incredibly time-sensitive. My new oncologist and I did not get along. I can be very descriptive of what I really thought about that doctor then, but I will be mild in my delivery on this one. The doctor had a blaming tone, so I had to overlook it. He and I looked about the same age. He was an type A in personality, and so was I. We bumped heads constantly but somehow managed to keep focused on getting me the care that I needed. Many times he would be rude and overbearing, and I would snap right back with a razor-sharp tongue. Harvey would sit there quietly as the doctor and I battled. It literally seemed that I had no voice and no support from anyone. The doctor screamed because the only thing he knew was that the situation was bad. Perhaps he really wanted to help, but from his training, all he knew was to lay out a platter full of chemo. At that point, I had gotten through without a whole heap of it. But I knew that these people would close the door and not help me if I did not do it their way.

As the doctor looked at the grossness of the tumors, it seemed obvious that he did not want to touch me. Did I have the plague? Was he going to catch the disease? That is what I felt. Harvey too seem very concerned. He looked at the spreading of the tumors and seemed broken. I saw in him a declining faith and a confidence that the end was near for me. This was a tough pill to swallow. Seeing and hearing the fear all around me was overbearing. Whenever I saw or heard the doubt in someone, it would light the fire within me to grab hold of something fused with hope. And that was God's Word.

I regretted what I observed in the people around me. I had to press forward though. I would not fire another doctor. I had to suck it up and drive on, as we often touted in the military. Suck it up and drive on! Take your eyes off of the overbearing doctor, and take your eyes off of disappointment and failed expectations in others, and focus on the outcome. We had to get these tumors to stop growing like this? I began to pray feverishly.

Lord, help me. This is too much for me to bear. You said for me to cast my cares upon you Lord. You said your yoke is easy and your burdens are light. Lord, take this burden off my neck and put it on your neck. Let me not, Lord, be overtaken with fear, for you said that you have not given me a spirit of fear, but a spirit that is sound, powerful and full of love. Give me strength, Lord. Help my ears to hear with clarity. Give me peace Lord that I may be able to function with clear purpose. I thank you Lord in advance for loving me. I thank you Lord for caring for me. I thank you Lord, that you said that the enemy cannot have me. I thank you, Jesus.

After praying, I remember a calmness came over me. I was able to think clearly amidst all the doubt, the fear from my collective family, the rudeness, and everything else that came out. I remembered again that this situation was not just about me. I knew that the challenges I had faced, and dealt with, centered around faith. The faith of the doctor, the faith of my dad, the faith of my mother, the faith of my grandmother, my aunts, my husband, and my friends....everyone displayed a difference here. What I saw in almost every person was fear in some form. Many had an ungrounded faith in something they knew nothing about...chemo that is. Many people yelled at me and scoffed at my choices. Many people wanted me to talk less of faith and just take the medicine. One day my mother called. She yelled and cursed at the top of her lungs. "Take the darn medicine"! she yelled. "We want you to live, and you are doing all these god-forsaken things that don't work. Take the darn medicine"!

During that period, I formally hired the Mederi staff in Ashland, Oregon to serve on my primary team to advise me. After they fully reviewed my case, the staff did a wonderful job in teaching me how to blend the chemotherapeutic medicine with a holistic approach to protect my vital organs. For the first time, I had an opportunity to work with Mederi in living color. I can't begin to tell you how they illuminated my soul. They did not tell a doom and gloom story, although they did say we had to move quickly and smartly. They insisted I redo all my tests so they could get their own baselines. My oncologist hated this. He kicked against this the whole way and made sure he articulated his feelings in his notes. It began to get personal, but I had to stay the course. He would be on my team, and Mederi would be on my team. Mederi had my first ear in that I tended to take their advice over that of anyone else. Their approach to cancer with a full understanding of main stream oncology and alternative care mixed with diet and spirituality was the perfect fit for me. Finally, I was able get explanations of why things were occurring in my body. This was in stark contrast to what my oncologist was offering. It made him uncomfortable, and he let me have it every time. That was okay though. I realized then that I had to remember that my life was my responsibility. And even with the pressures presented, I had to make decisions according to the leading and guiding of my Lord. With me, this process would be different from the norm. Somehow, God would turn this around. Somehow!!!

Mederi first asked me to get a sensitivity test administered so that we could determine the right type of chemo to take. Had it not been for Mederi, I would have perpetually been in a cycle of disagreeing with and firing my doctors. But Mederi taught me this....'do your best to keep a good relationship with your doctor. Your doctor does not have the benefit of knowing or understanding what we know. Most doctors are genuine and excellent in their craft, they simply follow what they have been taught. The staff at Mederi encouraged me, they would guide me into developing a good relationship with my doctors, so that they might benefit by my example.

I followed what Mederi advised, though tough and humiliating at times. I kept my doctors and had to let a lot of my angry pride down. I knew my oncologist had to take precautions based on the medical law. I asked for the sensitivity test, and it was clear he didn't know what it was. I got it cleared through the insurance company, and we proceeded forward. The surgeon assigned took a little more meat off the tumor as a biopsy and sent it in to pathology. Both the surgeon and Mederi got the results. Mederi recommended a particular chemo regimen, and I followed suit. I also took three additional marker tests that the oncologist was not privy too which allowed us to have additional information to help in determining which treatment to administer. Mederi also put me on a strict holistic plan which never hindered my chemo regimen. By following a combined team approach of traditional and holistic treatments, I was able to get over the hump for a while. At the end of the four-month cycle of aggressive chemotherapy including Taxatere, the tumor markers went down from over 350+ to 35. I was totally relieved that these monstrous bloody tumors had melted away before my very eyes. All of my team members were also glad. Maybe I could breathe for a while.

Maybe. Just maybe????

Chapter 4

The Fourth Time Around

The month was August, the very end of August, 2012. I thought that since the tumors had gone away, I should also stop the chemo. I remained on Herceptin though - a targeted hormone therapy that many women could live for decades on. This was interesting for me because I don't believe in chemo drugs, especially long term. I remembered Iraq. I remembered how mysterious it had been to pick up the same video twice, and to watch a video on the life and work about that doctor from Los Angeles who had worked for twenty years to get this Herceptin drug approved. The whole drug issue was still an area that I did not want to be totally dependent on. I would struggle with this issue continuously. Because I remained on Herceptin, I would have to take a heart test faithfully every ninety days to aggressively monitor my heart, since it was known to cause congestive heart failure.

In my heart and soul, I wanted never to have to take the drugs or be dependent on them. *Was there something wrong with me and my faith that I could not do this without the drugs? I struggled then. I had never before wavered in my faith. I wish I could just totally trust with all my might. But did I have it wrong somehow? Why was the Lord so precise in sending me that message that one night in Iraq?* That had been a clear message, no doubt. As time passed I had to constantly coach myself to trust those signs. Eventually, I would grow into this life lesson: to trust God in any situation, in every situation. With the drugs, I would trust God to have the drugs take care of the bad, while he protected me and preserved me in the interim. Even in the midst of seemingly greedy institutions, arrogant leaders, practitioners, and with all the politics of cancer, I would have to trust God. If I chose not to take the drugs, I would have to trust in that as well. If I lived, I would trust that I still possessed and owned my healing, despite the drugs and despite what my body looked like or felt. If I died from crazy complications or crazy side effects, I still would have to hold onto what was true. The truth is, no matter what I did and no matter if I lived or died, I still would possess my healing, that is what I believe!

Not that I speak in respect of want or need: for I have learned, in whatever state I am, to be content...

Philippians 4:11 (NKJV)

Later, I would run into a particular lady and her friend. I refer to them as the dynamic duo. I call them that because when you see one, you always see the other. They often call me on the phone to check on me. And they have interceded for me in prayer. I love them and sincerely appreciate Ms Sarah and Ms Reese. Ms Reese looked at me recently, and said "child, you don't look like nobody who has been sick." Her statement blessed me, because this disorder is not what I choose to own. My attitude is one where I own what God says, which is that *I am healed by his stripes*.

So my prayer has always been:

Lord, protect me against the harmful effects of man-made drugs. Let the drugs do what they are supposed to do. Protect my vital organs that I may be strong and live a life of quality. Let no harm befall me. As I go through the many conflicts with the doctors, please make my way straight. Lord, set it up so that when it is all said and done, you get the glory. Enable it Lord, that I see you in all things, and that my family friends and doctors see you. Let me be a living miracle.

Beloved, I pray that you may prosper in all things and be in health, just as your soul prospers...

3John 1:2 (NKJV)

After saying this prayer, I would thank the Lord for my healing. I would thank him for at least six more decades of life and I would keep it moving. This is a place I had to grow into. But before then, here is what happened the fourth and fifth time around. It happened quickly.

At the end of August 2012, I was feeling liberated after months of chemotherapy. It was time to move on with my life. My new full time job would be to resume the activities of President of Bryant Buchanan Productions. I would continue to write plays and present high end art programs for the community and nation. I love writing and producing theatrical shows.

A look back....I started my production company, Bryant Buchanan Productions Inc., seventeen years earlier after a dream in which I saw myself writing programs and plays, teaching about the gospel. I had been on active duty a number of years, was married and wanted to open a business. My husband and I had saved some money and began efforts in opening a food establishment. Just as we were about to launch, I began to have these clear dreams about playwriting and production. The dreams were so vivid, that it made me stop in my tracks and ask the question: "Are we about to make the right move in opening a food business"? I asked my husband to trust me. We stopped the idea of a food business and instead moved in the direction of producing plays. This move was a move of total faith. What was I thinking? I had no theatre training, but I was moving forward anyway? Wow. Even I questioned myself. But that inner voice inside pushed forward through an entire military career. I would take two years to prepare...research, forming a corporation and forming the foundation.

At that time in our lives, we fell under the spiritual leadership of Pastors Crosby and Rose Bonner. It was in their church I really began to open up to the spirit concerning worship, prayer and a stronger foundation in the Word. It was there, I would truly learn about the faith experience for the first time in my Christian walk. I loved my time there. I loved the worship experience, and I loved how the Word was taught. It was there, I would meet two of my greatest friends and supporters to this day: Evangelist Dr. Eve Taylor and Mrs. Willa Kynard, who became my prayer warriors and surrogate mothers, who would support me in all my life endeavors, just as my family did.

We as a corporate production company had our first gospel play at Lincoln theatre, Washington, DC before a capacity crowd, on opening night in 1997. Though there were serious technical issues that first night, we have grown and seen the potential of hundreds of artists over the years and have ministered to thousands all over the world with plays. Many would start as an artist, not knowing that they were really called to serve as disciples of the Lord. It was during these years that I began to realize my calling and faith was a little different than others. I began to realize some of what God was calling me to do. I met many challenges along the way with people who doubted the vision and who in their own way would try to thwart the delivery of God's Word, and try to stop me from working with others. But it was the Grace of God that I experienced all along, but didn't know it then. God provided for me in every single instance of acted out faith, now faith. Every instance, not some instances, but in every instance!!! As time went on, I began to grow in faith with grace. The pieces of the puzzle were coming together in every season of my life.

From that point, my family and I would travel the world, with the army as my primary job, and the production company followed everywhere we went. In each endeavor and experience it would take great faith to see the realization of every production. In every instance, we helped develop and pull out talent in every person we worked with. We were able to minister God's Word and the people in our productions went on to ministry themselves. I tell you this because this entire process started with a dream. Its inception, and the fruits of our labor-the production company took obedience and faith to accomplish. It took uncommon faith. I discovered this during my season with the beautiful Bonner family.

I eventually moved on to a 1-year hardship unaccompanied tour to Korea, in 2003 without my family. As the Lord would have it, I was divinely led to produce a new play that I had been saying I would write for a while. The play was about a fractured Christian family with the mom as the center focus. Here, the mom's faith would prove an integral factor in pulling the family together as she dies from cancer. In retrospect, it seemed interesting to me that I would write about a woman going through cancer before I experienced it myself. It was also strangely odd as to the bizarre events that took place as I wrote that particular play called "Mama, Mama, Oh Mema" (renamed to "When the Soul of a Woman Cries")in 2004. That year was a year of great personal revelation for me. I had high times in the Lord and great personal and professional success, but I also had some of the most heartbreaking moments of self reflection and failure. That was a year between God and I-totally, the only other time besides Iraq.

In January 2004, someone in the community church found out I was a professional playwright and had told our division chaplain. In my spare time from work, I trained in ministry under this chaplain, even though we were at the same military rank. He was my spiritual leader that year. He was a man of God who I liked very much. He was no-nonsense, he held us to a high standard of personal conduct which I liked. With him I felt safe, and I trusted him. The chaplain had a great respect for me also, and asked me to write a play. In my mind, I had planned on taking a break from plays for a year because I was a little burned out from work back at home. You couldn't convince me to do a major production in a foreign country without any known support. At least that is what I thought. After a little while, the Holy Spirit convicted me. I would begin having visions again. Once convicted, I knew I could no longer delay. I had to move out smartly, as it is commonly said in the military.

I knew I had to write the story. I gave myself five weeks to complete it. The fifth week approached, and I was in a crunch because I was not as close to being finished as I needed to be. The weekend came, and I had to get the script finished...there was no more time...it had to be completed. Distractions had to go, so I called a cab driver, or the adishee (spelling in hongul for a male worker) to take me to a water point. My adishee did not speak English, nor did I speak Hangul. I pulled out my book of Hangul and made some pretty bad attempts at describing a river, a lake. Somehow the adishee figured it out and began traveling far away from the camp. We would first go to a dried creek. I said, "no," while making hand gestures to keep looking for a body of water. The next stop would be a muddy river. "I said, adishee, "no--ooo. Come on, please find me a lake". Finally after the third try, the adishee found a huge lake in a far off place. I could tell he was worried and didn't want to leave me out in such a far off place as a black woman. He knew the community had not encountered people who looked like me. I paid him and gestured that I would be alright. He left, and then I began to focus. The distractions had been great, and I needed quiet. I needed time alone with the Lord to talk about how to finish this unnamed play. I found a place to sit on a bench facing the lake. It wasn't home, but it was a body of water and I had to work with it. I pulled out my Bible, play notes and outline. Just as I got into a rhythm, three strangers approached where I sat. Three Korean men sat around me. One stooped low to the ground and just stared. It was the c tom for Koreans to squat and stare. One man seemed to be about 75-80+ years, and the other two about 40. Nonetheless, they were tuned in, and it was clear that I was the stranger and they wanted to know who I was and what I was doing in their park. One man boldly touched my Bible. He knew what it was. I gestured, giving him permission to look at it. All three men began to speak to each other. They were asking questions, and I stopped writing and watched. They asked me questions but I did not understand, even with my interpretative book. In lieu of talking, I drew symbols to help them understand and showed them a picture of my family. They wanted to know my age, and I told them I was almost forty (I was thirty six). Somehow, they could not believe I was a grown woman with a husband and family. They wanted to know why I had my bible and what was I going to do with it. They were so intrigued, two men went off and gathered more people from other parts of the park. In an instance, what started with three people ended up being a mob of more than fifty people, squatting, talking, gesturing, touching, and questioning. It was like something out of time for me. I couldn't figure out where all the people came from. At some point, it felt like they were mobbing me, and fear crept in. I immediately pulled out my phone and called home. The time was about

1pm in Daegu, Korea and 3am at home in Georgia, U.S. Harvey picked up knowing there was a problem. He heard the panic in my voice, as I told him where I was and what was going on. He quickly eased my concern by telling me to close my eyes, pray and be still. I did just that and one by one the people stopped touching me and went away. The experience was intense as that had never happened to me before. I knew then that something was going on. Something was preventing me from getting this written product completed. I then picked up my gatherings and moved quickly away from the scattered mob. I moved to the edge of the lake which was separated by a fence. I stood at the fence under a gazebo. I told myself, you will complete this play today. I settled my mind and began to write. Next, a little bird flew at me and nipped my body. I thought it strange, but as soon as it occurred another bird nipped me and within seconds, another mob...now birds were attacking me. This time it was a flock of birds again numbering around fifty. I could not believe what was happening. I had no reactionary space to grab my phone for help, but I remembered what Harvey had told me to do. I did the same thing as before in praying the people away. So I stood still, absolutely still and called on the name of Jesus and prayed. I took the nips and little nudges from the birds, and it soon subsided. The atmosphere cleared within minutes. Once the bird mob ceased, I decided it was time to get the hell out of that place. Forgive my language, but I knew it was time to go.

I packed my things and I waived for a cab and got home before dark. I was baffled however. As I held my notes in my hand, I knew that there was something going on. Something was attacking me in the spiritual realm and it was manifesting in the natural. *What did God know about this play, about my life, about the impact of this play on other peoples' lives?* He knew something, and the devil knew it too. All along there had been distractions, to keep me from moving forward in my purpose. Over the next three days, I would find the time and focus to complete this piece on time. Major themes in the play would include restoring the family that has been dysfunctional, the dangers of self condemnation, and the truth about God's love. Over the years, many families have been delivered after watching this production. Here was another example of uncommon faith and God's Grace.

Recalling experiences like the aforementioned would prepare me for my fourth time going through cancer. As previously mentioned, the month was August, 2012. I had made the decision to stop the chemo and continue only with Herceptin. In September, I felt fine and looked fine. It appeared on the surface that my body was regaining its vitality. This would mean so much to me. I needed desperately to be able to function normally. How could I continue to manage all of the responsibilities as a wife in my home without vitality? How could I be an effective CEO without my vitality? The same question applied for ministry as a whole. So, during these times of intense inquiry and concern about how I was going to make it, I remembered the Lord's vision that he had given me. The vision for the future had not fully manifested, so that meant that I had to keep pressing forward.

Month two rolled by, and I was picking up my swag, if I may use these terms. My hair grew back. The side effects waned all the way down. I traveled less to the doctor. This was huge for me, as sometimes going to the doctor so often seemed stressful. The enormous time and energy spent in between those four medical walls seemed endless. It seemed once you were in, you were never going to leave. Insurance issues and medical bills became a regular member of my family and were fully embedded. If I wasn't going to see my oncologist, I was getting a scan, an echocardiogram, my bones checked, my eyes, ears, nose checked, my privates checked, everything!!. The treadmill was on full speed. I also had appointments with Mederi, which frankly were the only ones I looked forward to. At the Center, I got a breath of total truth. You know truth when you hear it. It feels different to the soul. There was no confusion. There was no inquiry. There was only peace and assurance. While I looked forward to meetings at Mederi, they were expensive. My savings were getting low. Medical bills were mounting and the business expenses were still aggressive. Nonetheless, we pressed forward. The third month rolled on, and I was flying high, feeling free. The feeling of freedom can't be understated.

One of the biggest challenges with someone going through a disorder for which the doctors say that there is no cure, is the fear of the disease returning. I can use the word concern over fear, but many are paralyzed by the thought of the disease spreading and/or returning. Also, both patient and family members alike often think of the worse, death. Dealing with one's own fears or concerns and absorbing that from others is a constant battle in the mind. It is critical to replace these thoughts, concerns and fears with the Word immediately. It is critical to understand that the biggest and best weapon against cancer is the Word. The bumps and tumors may form but **Isaiah 54:17(NKJV)** says **that "no weapon formed against me shall prosper."** They can never prosper against the Word of the Lord. This applies in life and in death. I say this because we all will die some day...our flesh will go back to dust. Somehow, someway, we will die in the flesh. Our spirit though never dies. **The spirit will return to the God who gave it... Ecclesiastes 12:7 (NKJV).** So I believe that no matter what may come of the flesh to move you closer to that transition, you should keep your spirit rooted in the Lord.

Divine permanent healing is yours, forever, in life and in death. **For to die in the Lord is gain... Philippians1:21(NKJV).**

So when November, 2012 finally came, I remember painting my nails bright red. I painted them red, and as I placed my finger on my blank chest, I immediately noticed another swelling. This was my greatest concern. After all this time with multiple recurrences, I was now hypersensitive to every lump and bump on my body. This time, it started as a very small raised mound on my right chest wall. *What is this, I asked? Is the cancer returning? Or did it ever really go away?* I thought the chemo had cut right through and got it all out? Or did it? And what exactly does the chemo do anyway? Is it feeding the cancer? What the heck is going on? So, I took my red-painted nail and placed it on my chest to begin a record. Each day, I would photograph myself by placing my red-painted nail against the slow growing tumor. I needed to know if I was going to go through again? And the answer was yes. Over the next couple of weeks, I compared the pictures as the tumors were growing back, and even more aggressively. It was like we had fed my body some weed-killer for a few months, but now I was sprouting new tumors and new growths like weeds. My lawn was soon full, plush, green and ready to be cut.

I went to the oncologist yet again and we argued again back and forth. We were both frustrated and angry. I was angry at him and the entire institution of medicine. "Why did I let those people cut my breast off"? I screamed. My instincts went all the way back there. It had not seemed right, nor normal and decent then, and now the same feelings returned. I had been told that if I got my breast and the areola cut off via a mastectomy, the cancer would be gone. Of course, you know I also had been given the usual disclaimer...it may be gone, no guarantees. I had been told and believed those long courses of chemo were my best chance of cure. That too was not true for me. Now, I felt even more confused as I now had a myriad of new/continued tumors. So what was I to do now. I had had multiple biopsies, a lumpectomy, a mastectomy, a failed breast reconstruction and multiple courses of chemotherapy and radiation therapy. *What was I to do now?* At this point, I truly did not trust the institution of medicine. I was really mad at it all.

Chapter 5

The Fifth Time Around

I was mad at the doctors. I was mad at the institution of medicine, and the overall options or lack of options. In my soul, I felt there was more. There had to be more. I felt as though the healthcare system of our nation called the United States of America, was gripped inside of an ugly maze of greed. I believed that people were dying because of a refusal to change the educational process of how our doctors are trained, and I believe that we as a society are hooked on drugs, ourselves and not reliant on God. This is one of the terrible truths of how Satan has a grip... through misappropriation of drugs and greed. This would be my struggle. I prayed-

"Lord, help me find a better way. My illness is spreading like wildfire. I don't know what else to do. The doctors don't know what to do. They are well intended. They too had trusted in the medical school process only to discover some serious failings to our nation's medical process.

So I prayed even more.

"Lord, help me to find the truth. Help me to navigate, and to get to where I need to go. Guide me. Protect me. Keep me from being gripped by fear. These tumors are growing fast across my chest. What do I do"?

As I spoke to my doctor, yet again he blamed me for getting off the drugs. Most doctors would agree with him. My freedom had lasted for only four months, and now I was back to the drawing board. What do I do now? I had told the oncologist, I needed time to think. His recommendation at that point was to call in a surgeon and to cut into my chest cavity. Now imagine this, my chest was already mutilated and flat. There were new boils forming, bleeding and big. There were about seven boils growing out from my chest wall. They were gross. Most people could not stomach the view. Harvey was very concerned, poor guy. He was suffering too. I just couldn't believe it. I adamantly refused to let someone cut into my chest again. That would mean skin grafts, and only God knew what else. Because there was so much tension, I had to go away and think. I had to leave and just get quiet. Now, I had complained over the prior months that my oncologist had never physically touched my breast and examined me. It seemed strange to me that during my follow-up visits, checkups were only done by checking my blood work and by reading on a computer. He had checked my breast only twice in the entire time I had known him. I thought this odd. My previous oncologist had always examined or checked my breasts. Perhaps I had the plague. Perhaps he was uncomfortable. But whatever the reason, the records revealed that he routinely never checked my breasts. At some point, I began also to feel a mass in my left breast. In the five years of dealing with this disease, I had not had a problem with my left side, nor had the cancer spread anywhere in my body. I asked the doctor to please hear my new concerns. Our relationship was strained. I could have let this doctor go, considering our poor relationship and considering he wasn't paying any attention to the signals. His pride and arrogance remained thick. Mine was thick with him, and I feverishly prayed each time I visited him, because I wanted our relationship to be better. I wanted him to see the God in me, but he often saw the darker side because he would just piss me off most times.

For some reason, which baffles me to this day, I did not let him go. I knew, he and I had to get our relationship together. My husband was always present, but being non-confrontational, never spoke up to the doctor. This time was crucial, and I felt boxed in. I told my oncologist that I would take forty days to pray and to determine the way ahead. I would come again after I got clarity. Of course, people think you are nutty when you say you are going off to pray for forty(40) days. At that point, I didn't care what anyone thought. I cared only what the Lord thought. Deep in my spirit and soul, I knew God would get the glory from this maze of craziness. He would do the delivering, with or without the drugs, with or without the surgery, with or without life. At the end of the day, he owns all the cattle on the hill, he rules the world, he has complete control over everything. **His Grace would be Sufficient.**

Because I had felt this new thing on my left breast, I went to my primary care physician. She was my assigned angel. Her dad was a naturopathic doctor, so she understood both worlds: naturopathic and mainstream medicine just by her upbringing. She immediately checked my chest and breast and realized the urgency of the right chest wall with the recurring formations of tumors in this fourth overall occurrence. But her gut was highly suspicious of my left breast as well. She scheduled my appointments through her medical chain. I saw a whole chain of different doctors who worked down the hall from my primary oncologist. Before leaving her office, she asked me what did I want to do about the left side, as it was progressing. I told her I had to clear my head. Let me pray. Let me think. I told her about my 40 day prayer period. I was about 20 days in at this point. She understood because she too was a Christian.

That same week, I took all the tests one could take in one day. I had the MRI, a full body PET scan, and my left breast was biopsied.

As I sat inside the all too familiar dark room with the pictures of my left breast illuminated, full and beautiful, I thought back to 2008 at the Airforce base on Cocoa Beach, Florida. That was the first time I had seen this type of equipment. Unfortunately, I was now very familiar with the process.

The female doctor presented the news as if it was the first time all over again. "Ms. Buchanan, I'm sorry to tell you, that you may have cancer again. I have seen a lot of patients, and I have never seen anything quite like this. I have compared your previous records and scans. I am surprised that your cancer has taken so long to spread to your left breast. But today, the pictures show that the cancer is all in your chest wall from left to right. And, the new cancer in your left breast was not there one month ago, because I checked. I checked the work of your other doctors and there was no cancer then. But now that there is something new, you must act now. Your situation has so progressed, you must do something now." The doctor had put in overtime with me and made concessions to open up numerous previous tests. She was concerned that my oncologist had overlooked the mass, as we all were. I had a comfort level with her and I knew that she meant well. We sat in the dark room face to face. It was late in the day, early evening in fact. The doctor had asked me to wait until she had finished her rounds so we could have some private time. She too was a breast cancer survivor and wanted to speak to me, woman to woman. We sat in the room in an intimate, friendly manner. She told me that she recommended getting another mastectomy for the left breast to get at the core of the matter. She told me that she had had a double mastectomy when she learned she had the Brac1 gene. I listened as she asked me what did I want to do? I respected this woman, but life had revealed some things to me and taught me a lot. I no longer believed that a mastectomy would get at the core of things.

Besides, it left me feeling mutilated without a guarantee of cancer cure. It did not seem to be humane. This is my personal view, my direct life experience, it is what I experienced and believe. I would choose another route. I had to depend on the Lord to show me that route, and then I would rest in that decision. Prior to meeting with this female physician, I had stumbled upon an accredited doctor in New York, who did laser surgery as an option for breast cancer treatments- the only one in the country apparently at that time. I researched him thoroughly and developed a sense or a leading to move in that direction. So as I sat next to this genuine female doctor, my heart could not be turned her way. Some would call it sheer stubbornness. But there was something in my soul that would not let me go down the same road to Abilene with getting another of my breast cut off via a mastectomy. I just couldn't do it. I politely hugged the doctor who had passionately done her job. She, along with my primary care provider, had taken charge when they saw my most recent problem. They had rapidly gotten me tested, provided the needed information for me to now go and make the necessary decisions for my life. They had done their jobs, now it was my turn to prayerfully navigate the next move. I said goodbye to the doctor. As I left, she made one more plea. She said, "Ma'am, if you don't take the next steps, you will die. I've never seen anything like this before. Please have a mastectomy, begin aggressive radiation and chemotherapy now."

Okay, that was one option, but God showed me another. I explained to the kind doctor as gingerly and as respectfully as I knew, that I would try something different. I also explained that God will help guide me. She marveled at me, and I likewise marveled at her.

> **Life point:** In cases, like this you have to know that often when the world says and thinks one way, God may think and say things differently.

I had been told I was going to die by the world, but God had said, ***I will not die, but I shall live, and declare the works of the Lord...Psalms 118:17 (NKJV).*** How about that? How about, ***not all illness is unto death...*****John 11:4 *(NKJV).*** How about, ***I thank you Lord, for by your stripes I am healed...*****Isaiah 53:4-5 (NKJV).**

And do not be conformed to this world: but be transformed by the renewing of your mind, that you may prove what is good, and acceptable, and the perfect will of God...

Romans 12:2 (NKJV)

Life question...so what would you do if the traditional healthcare system told you to go in the only known direction of surgery, even if that way wasn't guaranteed? What if that system put so much pressure on you to do it, even if it did not correlate with your belief system? What would you do? Could you stand, and defy the system if your life was on the line? Could you push through all the opinions of others and strong admonitions of the so-called experts? What would God think if you did? At the end of the day, whom would you trust ?

I left the office knowing that the doctor thought I was making the wrong decision. As much as I liked her, my instincts were guiding me in another direction. My life depended on it. Of course, dealing with the doctors was not my only challenge. I had family rumblings, and they were loud and persistent. My mother screamed at me constantly. My husband panicked, it was rough for him seeing me go through this yet again, and I knew it would only heighten. My grandmother gingerly made comments. My aunt kept quiet, though her quietness was loud. My dad reacted in the same manner as my husband-in panic and fear mode...bless their hearts. Other family members would visit as if they were paying their last respects. Wow. They all loved me. They all wanted the best for me. And each person in their own way wanted me to stay within the mainstream healthcare system. It was all they knew. What I knew, was that I had tried all the traditional approaches to my cancer. My soul instinct said there was more. My soul instinct still says it.

A few weeks passed, and I began to get more and more clarity in prayer. I got peace with the decision to go to New York and have both issues addressed there using laser therapy with Dr. Vincent Ansanelli. He is a superb doctor with over 45-years experience in laser surgery as an option for the treatment of breast cancer. He was the only surgical oncology doctor doing laser breast surgery as far as I knew. Dr Ansanelli had trained with Dr Kaplan one of the first surgeons who used the carbon dioxide laser in general surgery. Dr. Ansanelli's surgical treatment options have been questioned over the years, as he extended this therapeutic option as an alternative to a total mastectomy. He persevered and now has the respect needed from the medical community and thousands of clients whose breasts and lives he has he has helped to save. The bill would be extensive and be an out-of-pocket expense as this would be considered out of network and the laser treatment was non-traditional. Fortunately, I had the funds and would be able to make this sacrifice for my life.

Prior to the trip, I completed all of the preoperative paperwork. I also forwarded all of my previous scans and records for Dr Ansanelli to review prior to my arrival. Each doctor and his/

her staff in Georgia and New York, worked tirelessly to help get me situated over the next two weeks. My primary care doctor respected and supported my decision. It was time to go on another journey--the tide had shifted yet again.

January 2013 came, and it was time for Harvey and me to fly to New York. We knew we had shifted into a new place-spiritually and physically as soon as we stepped on the flight pad. I called on the name of Jesus as soon as we felt the freezing fingers of sheer cold grip our bodies. We immediately and literally ran for our friend called heat to cover every available patch of skin. As I began to run, I remember falling flat on the ground. I did not fall because of ice on the ground. I fell because something in my body had failed. For the first time on this treadmill of cancer, something different and new had begun. Harvey reacted fast and assisted me in getting up, asking me what had happened, as puzzled as I. "I'm not sure," I replied. "It was as though my legs just went out of service all of a sudden from under me." Neither of us knew what to do, except to take it slow and to pull me up to try and get me moving. Whatever had caused me to fall, and whatever the pain, it soon subsided and I was able to move again. Freezing, we moved with immense and concentrated purpose.

We were greeted by an entourage of loving family members; my dad, Bobby, uncle Pat, aunt Goldie, uncle Larry and my forever friend, operations manager and prayer warrior- Sharon Buntin. They had all stopped their busy schedules to meet with Harvey and me at our New York hotel. The first thing uncle Pat did when he saw me, was hug me and he put cash in my hands. What a love offering? He didn't know it, but I so appreciated this kind gesture. The mere fact he was there, was a blessing times a million.

The family then repositioned ourselves, and we all met at the Long Island clinic. What was funny was the reaction of the administrative nurse who saw us standing in the parking lot. Uncle Pat and aunt Goldie were dressed to impress, New York style in the midst of the cold winter. They looked good with their fur hats and coats. Harvey and I didn't care, we were so cold we just covered up anyway we could. Uncle Larry and Sharon stayed close to me like glue. The receiving administrator would see this gaggle of folks and would make a bold assumption. She immediately called her daughter, as she looked out the window looking at us in this all Jewish community and told her daughter, I believe the Jehovah witnesses are here to preach to us. She would tell me this story some time later, and I found it amusing, even today looking back. She made the comment, because the community apparently did not have any blacks gathering in the parking lot at anytime, especially that early in the morning. Needless to say, I would soon meet the medical staff. Dr. Ansanelli was an older Jewish doctor who was polite, direct and seemed very wise to me. His daughter worked at the front office and had a colorful New York attitude-confident, strong and full of energy. From the pictures on the wall, she had been a New York ballet star. The pictures were beautiful and stunning. It always amazes me to meet people and to learn their background.

My new doctor had a rich history in the area, full of proud contributions from his family members. The staff was friendly and began prepping me right away. When the doctor was ready to make his first on-the-spot evaluation, he displayed obvious shock at the progression of tumor formations on the right side of my chest. He was so shocked at what he saw that he kept repeating that my condition was very serious. He was extremely candid, and I could tell that he was worried. He immediately told me that laser surgery would not be the solution for my right side. My heart wanted to sink at that very moment because I had traveled so far, and I just knew within myself that I was supposed to be there.

He then stated that aggressive treatment with chemotherapy would be the immediate solution for the right side. He wished that I had gotten to him before the mastectomy because there could have been better options. He didn't believe that my right chest wall needed to look like that. In the meantime, he shifted his focus to the newly developed breast mass on the left side. He confirmed that he could in fact work with the left breast. He talked me through the plan for the day. We would spend the day getting this mass removed. The entire amazing day was a same day process. It would not harm my body image, instead it preserved my body image and got rid of the tumor seamlessly. After the laser process, I felt no pain, and my left breast had been preserved.

As we wrapped up the day, the doctor would counsel me on several fronts. He stated that the first priority was to treat my right side aggressively. He emphasized that he had not seen that level of tumor formation. While it may appear as if this doctor was unconventional, he was every bit able in his craft, experienced with conventional cancer treatments as well. I trusted him. I valued him. And although I felt some kind of way about the use of drugs, I knew I had to take action for a very real and present problem. I would have to make a decision, and I would have to take action now. His testimony and immense concern helped me to make the next intelligent decision for myself.

Life point: I have come to the realization that we all make decisions differently, for the bible tells us that all things are permissible, but not everything is beneficial...1Corinthians 10:23(NKJV). I have always believed that each person has to have peace and confidence present when deciding what is right for the individual situation. When I have peace within, there is a calmness in the process. There is a confidence and assurance in the midst.

The doctor advised that I should take a few months to get the right chest tumors under control and then return. "I may, be able to have some skin to work with to clean up the area," he said. I thought to myself, Lord Jesus, now you know...you will have to provide the money for that. This was to be a yeoman's feat with respect to my savings. *Lord, you would have to provide from this point.* I knew from experience this would mean, I would have to work even harder with my business. I could not be broke and have the best healthcare.

Dr Ansanelli also spoke to me about how happy he was, that I was there. He specifically stated that he rarely gets clients of color, and asked that I be an advocate to inform African-Americans about this option. I knew that this would be my pleasure.

I left that day with my lovely family; Harvey, uncle Larry, Sharon, uncle Pat, aunt Goldie and my dad. I so appreciate them and love them. I can't thank them enough for their love, time and support. And that love offering -wow! The fellowship we shared that weekend, crying, laughing and eating in that New York hotel was incredible.

I would return home to Georgia soon after. As I maneuvered through the airports, I would have a couple more episodes of falling completely out. I didn't know what else to do but to go to my doctor immediately. My oncologist would have a quiet attitude at my next visit . Initially, he made comments with regards to his disapproval of my decision to proceed with laser surgery for my left breast. I certainly didn't appreciate the stares from the staff and was offended initially. All eyes were on me. The whispers were loud and offensive. Although, I had not told the nurses about my trip, many of them knew of the details because the doctor had said something in a case meeting to them. They commented on my personal choice to do something different, non-traditional. I knew my choice been a good one, the right one for me, even though they didn't understand. I felt at that point like the woman from the Scarlet letter or even the woman with the issue of blood. They all made me feel like I had done something wrong.

The clinic was a family atmosphere, so chatter existed. I resented the fact that people judged me for a decision so personal, and life-impacting. I often wondered, what would the doctor do if he were faced with such a challenge? What would he propose for his own family member? Why was he talking about my trip to New York with the staff? My disposition wasn't pleasant with all of this. Of course, the lioness poked her head and roared a couple times, but I quickly settled down. There was no time. I had to focus on my right breast and also figure out why I was falling out.

My oncologist would immediately send me back to a partnering doctor to get further tests to scan my entire body for cancer. Meanwhile, the bouts of falling out still occurred sporadically. I still remember preparing to see the partnering doctor to review my X-ray results. I had to travel to another clinic in the city for that service. The staff was very nice and cordial. I distinctly remember praying days prior and listening to my Mederi CD's. I remember just prior to going to that appointment, I began to get quiet messages and signals of the impending news. This seemed to be a recurring trend with God. Whenever some sort of bad news was coming my way, he would graciously find a way to prepare and to calm me. The Lord reminded me that regardless of the news, even in the worst case scenario, I was to trust his Word, and trust what He had revealed to me. I was reminded that I still have work to do and so I should not waiver in trusting Him. "*Not so, Shatrece! The devil cannot have you. No matter what you hear, plant your feet, stand tall, accept the news, keep your faith and move forward in life.*" These were the instructions I got from the Lord in the days before getting the news from the doctor. It was like going through day one all over again, but I had to stand on the deliberately delivered Word of the Lord. Harvey and I sat in the doctor's office waiting for the nurses and the doctor to return. I felt they were stalling. I stepped into the hallway looking for the young doctor. It was apparent he was not accustomed to giving bad news. The nurses looked sad and pale. I asked them to please get the doctor so that we could move forward. Finally, I greeted the doctor and told him that it was alright. "I can take whatever you say. Let's get started." There were four people in the room...Harvey, the doctor, the nurse and me. The doctor began speaking and stated that my experiences with the falling out was as a result of the cancer spreading throughout my body. He explained that I now had -Stage 4 breast cancer, and that it was terminal. I could tell, it was extremely difficult for this young doctor to explain this to me. I felt badly for him. Because the Lord had already braced me for this information, I did not respond in the way everyone else expected. The nurse looked grim and sad. The doctor looked like he was going to cry, and Harvey was in a state of reserved shock and grief. As I looked around the room at all the fear, I decided I would not take that approach. The Lord had prepared me. I was going to follow his lead and listen to God versus yielding to the negative report. At that point, I spoke to those in the room. First, I told the doctor, "Sir, don't worry, everything will be alright. You can tell me all that you need to tell me. I can take it. And now, what is the way ahead? We need a plan of action." The nurse looked awestruck. She perhaps thought I was going to break down and fall out crying, and was shocked at my overall demeanor. At that point, the doctor, who was a surgeon by the way, said that what we needed to do is to perform surgery on my right chest to get control of the tumors. I listened to him carefully but a loud signal rang out immediately within me. I knew to trust those signals. I replied, "So let's get this straight. You want to cut the tumors out of my chest from a chest wall that is already flat? Wouldn't this be akin to scooping the insides of a cantalope?" The people in the room gasped in shock, that I would ask such a question. Before the doctor could respond, I said, "with all due respect, I will not let that happen". I was not going to allow my body to undergo that type of trauma again (considering I had already had a mastectomy which had already mutilated my body). To do that again but now deep into my chest cavity, that I would not allow. The decision was easy for me. The answer to that course of action was a resounding NO. We would have to go another route. The whole purpose of going to New York and spending my savings was to select a procedure with the least amount of trauma to the body, while holding the greatest amount of benefit in preserving my breast while minimizing future cancer reoccurrences. Laser surgery had done that for me. A cantaloping procedure did not fit this criteria, my criteria. Once I had made that decision, I was at peace. I cannot profess to having made all of the right turns in this process, but I can profess that the Lord has kept me, preserved me and guided me all of the way.

Just before leaving the clinic, the nurses would corner us in the hallway...there were several of them. They had been chattering with each other about my response to the news. They all marveled at my response and had never experienced that before. I really didn't understand it at first, but I see it clearer now. When you are someone who walks in faith despite the odds, that shocks people a bit when you really walk your faith out. To me, it was either depend and remember all the signals and signs of God to hold on and to press forward, or I could yield to the terminal tones of death and destruction. The nurses were encouraged and commented that they would never forget that day. I too was encouraged by them. I was reminded at that moment, that this journey of cancer wasn't just about me. It was about the Jesus in me. My approach to life as I walked through this trial with this cancer was that Jesus would get the glory at every step. It was about the fact that we now live under the dispensation of grace and that everything we do is by faith. It is ultimately about the gospel in the person of Jesus Christ who died for the remission of our sins, my sins. It is about the message of the gospel, which is the good news regarding the life, death and resurrection of Jesus Christ. At the end of the day, it is about me fully trusting in God and accepting all the benefits he has for me, which I have to pray out and walk out by faith. And through all of this, I've learned that every step of the way, God has already given me what I need, **for His Grace is Sufficient**...

After leaving the clinic, I soon returned to my oncologist. After he realized the cancer had spread, we immediately stopped all the foolish prideful attacks and shifted our focus. He exhibited genuine concern and insisted I be hospitalized. He questioned me fiercely and wanted to know more about the falls. He knew within himself he needed to make sure the cancer had not penetrated my spinal cord. His experience knew that this would be troublesome. I allowed him to hospitalize me to undergo yet more tests. In the transition, I remember I had to sit in a wheelchair because my legs were getting weaker. I felt as though I was going down the long hallway of shame, as I rolled passed all of the nurses and staff who seemed to look at me pitifully. Now I will admit, the feelings I had were not so much of God at this time, but of sheer pride. As I rolled down the hallway looking at the many people I had grown to like, I whispered to myself, I am getting out of this "blankety blank" chair. I refused to stay in this state.

So what do you do when your body is going through and your mind is fighting against what going on? How do you maneuver such an ordeal, when the situation appears to be spiraling out of your control? Something was growing inside of me, the root of something that no one could figure out. The days in the hospital proved that my spinal cord had not been impacted, but it meant we had to put a treatment plan together fast to prevent this possibility from becoming a reality. My oncologist and I actually had a turn in our relationship during that hospitalization. I had been praying for almost a year for our relationship to improve. I had so wanted to fire him multiple times, but the Lord never let my foolish pride prevail. I would get convicted every time I saw him, and would stay in place.

In the meantime, I remember meeting a beautiful nurse with long auburn hair. She and I got along well. When I looked at her name plate, I noticed she had the same name as my oncologist. Of course, I asked the question...do you know my doctor, Dr H? She pleasantly snapped back and said, "of course I do, that's my husband." I chuckled inside and said, wow, was this coincidence or is this another sign? I knew better than to think it was a coincidence. *Ok, Lord, what's next?* I asked the beautiful nurse-wife, "so tell me, how is your husband at home? You know, he gives me the blues and we are not getting along." The lovely woman then sat down and explained that normally, her husband leaves his work at work, but for some reason, he talks about you (meaning me) at home. The nurse called me by my first name, and stated that her husband really cares about me. She told me that he had been distraught when I developed the new bouts of falling. He had wanted to get care for me immediately. I trusted this beautiful lady. She was nice inside and out, which is what made her beautiful. Meanwhile, I had a request for her, and asked her "Please could you encourage your husband to be a little nicer to me, and to not talk over me in the office." I was very candid with her, and I know I took liberties with her because I believed she would communicate my concerns directly to her loved one better than any other person could. I needed this doctor. And truth be told, I believed he needed me. For the sake of the whole, we needed to get along. I believed in my soul that this experience was bigger than he and I. And to tell the whole story in order that others might be blessed, we had to stay together, work together and get along. Deep, deep down inside I knew there was a greater cause, a greater purpose to this process. My doctor was a part of that cause, so I had taken the liberty to speak with his wife. Unconventional I know, but it was necessary. We both needed peace and a clear direction.

Each morning in the hospital, I would watch my Christian shows like Creflo Dollar, Joyce Meyers, and Bobby Womack... and I would read and pray. My doctor would come in some time during or after, faithfully. It seemed he made it a point to visit me first. We both were cordial and polite. I do remember us having a heart to heart talk expressing that we both would do better in not cutting each other off and getting along. He also expressed that he was really concerned about me and about my well-being. I appreciated his words and remembered what his wife had said. Because of her, I believed him and I thanked God for our new relationship.

In the course of dealing with all the doctors, limited options and failed progression in many cases, patients often grow distrusting of the system. When diagnosed with a disorder, patients want to trust and believe that their doctors are all knowledgeable. Patients want to believe that the entire healthcare system and pharmaceutical system will do us right and guide us correctly. We trust that every doctor and nurse is ordained and called for a divine purpose, with a passion in their heart. We want to believe, that all the answers to our issues will be made available. The truth is, this isn't always entirely true. First, our doctors don't know everything. Oftentimes, they are learning by trial and error. Second, as elaborate as our nations' healthcare system is, we haven't figured everything out...that's why new discoveries are coming out every day. As far as pharmaceuticals, well let's just say I'll save my comments about this system for another book. In the meantime, we as patients come in hopeful, with an expectation that is wide open. This is not always being met fully or reciprocated. So when I broach the idea of trusting another doctor who is presenting treatment options to me that have harmed me, I am immediately on the defensive.

When I met my Dr. H, I had already been around the track a few times. I was no longer open to certain treatment options, out of concern for my whole person.

After getting released from the hospital, I told Dr H., I was going to call all of my stakeholders and put them around a table to help me determine the way ahead. While he did not like that, he indulged me, and we moved forward. My decision strategy and style had not changed. The challenge I've always had with this cancer journey is that the mainstream health system only presents limited options and then they say "that's all that is out there." We have to prayerfully discover what the other available options are. For me, laser surgery was an example of this. Mederi clinic was another example of this. Ask Martha Stewart, she invited Donald Yance of Mederi to her show twice and was amazed at the things that she didn't know. And we know Ms. Stewart is very well informed on a myriad of life issues. Suzanne Summers' book called 'Knockout' is another wonderful resource of information on cancer. And even your local health store contains a storehouse of heavenly discoveries.

Overall, my belief is this. God made everything on earth. He made a thousand cattle on a hill. He created the planets, the sky, the land the animals,...everything. He made everything for man. He even made food for our nutrition, and he made things to help us live. It is up to man to discover his blessings. It is my firm belief that cancer should be managed with a multi-faceted approach; not just set to chemotherapy, radiation and surgery-by knife. Effective cancer treatment should be supplemented by:

- a targeted diet with the proper seasonings (red, yellow, orange colored seasonings, plant based drinks, no dairy, organic foods, and lots of vegetables);

- sufficient exercise;

- a stress-free life;

- use of essential oils, balancing hormones; and

- small dose targeted therapies, and immunotherapy to name a few.

Of course dependence and development of a strong faith in God forms the foundation for all of the above.

For me, my continual prayer is...

Lord, protect me and guide me through this maze of medical confusion and chaos. Quickly reveal the truth to me, so that I may see clearly. Have me to trust in you more, than others. Continue to bless our medical community, that they may help your people and not harm them. Bless the doctors, give them wisdom and give them courage to always do what is right. Give them a heart for your people that they might serve with compassion. Lord, also bless my body, as I go through the various test and procedures. Protect my liver, protect my heart. Let no harm befall me as your Word says. Let no weapon formed against me prosper. If that weapon comes in the form of food, air, toxins, drugs, people or even unseen dangers, protect me Lord and preserve my life that I may do your will. In the name of Jesus, I pray. Amen.

Once the stakeholders came together, we agreed on Abraxene to get the tumors under control. Mederi had recommended this, as did Dr. H. I took the chemo and even a little radiation in the time period following my discharge. Mederi gave me holistic supplements to ensure that my liver was protected. And the protocol they used did not adversely impact my chemo regimen. Mederi ran many other tests as well. There researchers reviewed every cancer study in our country, they knew every new drug coming out of the FDA plus they knew how to mix this with their herbal protocol safely and efficiently. They also had the knowledge of innovative techniques in other countries. They recognized the seriousness of my condition and were fully committed to working with my oncologist as a team to provide forward progress. For me, this was the ideal way to go. I had every important component in place around me for a holistic approach to this cancer: my spirituality, my mainstream health care, diet, and physical activity plan-all combined. This worked for me---a total body approach.

The next several months would show immense improvement. My marker levels began to decrease. As the months went by, I got better. Within six weeks, I was able to get up and resume walking. I was determined. I received radiation therapy to my back and to my shoulders. As I began to get better, I noticed the tumors were all decreasing in size. But the aggressive chemo was another story. It was wearing me down, even though I had resumed a busy lifestyle with restarting one of my plays. The side effects were persistent with the nose bleeds, high blood pressure, weight gain, insomnia, heightened anxiety/ jitteriness, loss of all hair, eyebrows and all. Through all of this, the radiation side effects were also bad. There was nausea, burned skinned which turned black and a lot of spitting by the bottle full....tall bottles. Sometimes it was hard to sleep out of concern for choking on my spit. After a while, I felt I had to stop the radiation. From time to time, Dr. Ansanelli from New York would call to check on me. That was love to me. I had Mederi on my team, although it was getting tough to keep up with their expenses. Eventually, they would give me a scholarship to ensure I continued to get the assistance I needed.

Herein lies the issue for many of us...it is just so hard to pay for treatment options outside that of the mainstream recommendations. Even inside of our traditional healthcare system, paying for medical care gets tough with or without insurance or especially with inadequate insurance. It takes money and medical insurance to be and stay well in this country. Mine was getting thinner and thinner. But God would have to supply. **His Grace is Sufficient.**

By mid-year 2013, I was in full gear with the business of producing another one of my plays. This did me good. It kept me focused on something very positive and it kept me from going into any type of depression while sitting at home. I spent my days working with my operations manager-Sharon, my staff from Missouri, Renee, Tamika and Charles Sr.- my chief of staff. Shirley was another team member from North Carolina, who was a great supporter as well. She had lost her mother from cancer some years prior. Her heartbeat was to be a care provider. I worked with my team during the day, to prepare for rehearsals at night with the cast of "When the Soul of a Woman Cries." Working with the cast was amazing. It did so many things for me. It kept me functional. Others marveled at how I could work through my disorder. But the disorder did not define me. I defined it. I would work. I would still contribute to my community. I was not going to restrict myself to my bedroom. I needed to live my best life. Others would see this. Despite how I looked on the outside, I was still going to press forward and grab what the Lord said was mine...healing, peace, and wholeness. So while I was bald with no eyelashes and going through hot flashes like crazy, I persevered. We had a show to put on that November and the following January, 2014. As the year progressed, we as a cast had our two plays. Oftentimes, people saw the intensity of the side effects of the drugs, yet they still saw me working every day. I essentially wanted them to see me pressing through every life situation. Working with the young people and aspiring actors and singers continued to encouraged me, they kept me focused and alive. God blessed me with a gift, and I was going to use it until the day I died. He continually blessed me financially as well, I was going to use that for the advancement of his kingdom and to bless others. Even if it meant spending my last. My intent is to be a continual blessing to my community before I go on to eternity. My intent is to continue to encourage the next brother or sister to live their best life in Christ, despite the present circumstance.

I work within my given calling to stay alive because I know the Lord will take me home only when my work here is completed.

To my direct community, I would say this. We should continue to work with each other in harmony to advance our people. We should: put down hard pride; put down jealousy; put down racism; put down doubt; put down division; put down covetousness; put down greed; put down mistrust; put down self -exaltation and put down verbal attacks and slander. We should instead put on love, peace, and joy as we unify in this kingdom business. People are hurting all over the world. The world needs our leadership; and the church and community must do better. The church can help by coming together with itself and putting the unique gifts and talents together for the good of the community. If we don't, we will keep losing our precious saints to the world system. We should come together, work together and support one another!

After many months on the chemo regimen, the year ended. It was now 2014. All of my stakeholders were pleased, I had made it over the hump and the tumors had subsided. In my mind, I asked God to really get at the root of this cancer. I knew then and still know that the chosen protocols are keeping the cancer at bay. At the top of the year, Mederi ran more tests and after review, they advised that I should discontinue the heavy artillery of drugs and switch to a brand new drug called TMD1. They explained that it was a targeted therapy that would work with Herceptin to block off a dominant protein in my body(the simplified explanation). They further emphasized that my body no longer needed the heavy artillery of drugs that it had been getting. This new protocol would be administered every three weeks, in smaller dosages and it would only target the bad cells(cancer cells) in my body. I broached the subject with my oncologist. He disagreed with the recommendation to change. I requested a three way meeting to have him speak to Mederi. It did not happen. My oncologist had done everything right in the traditional system in providing my chemo treatments, protecting his interests and protecting his license. Here is the dilemma I had, Mederi had posed a legitimate option within the parameters of the mainstream, FDA standards but my mainstream doctor did not want to give it time or thought. Six months passed, and the tumor on my back grew according to my next PET scan. It was at that point, my oncologist came to me excited in telling me about a new drug, Kadclya. When he described the new drug, he described exactly what Mederi had announced just six months prior. I called the doctor out on this and barked. He admitted it was the same drug and said at least we caught it now. Essentially, Mederi had been right earlier. This is the reason, I like Mederi because they are a research foundation for both mainstream and unconventional cancer treatment options. They continuously evaluate the latest cancer research, in the U.S. as well as internationally, and they fully integrate a truly holistic approach to managing cancer to prevent it from overwhelming you. They do use a multifaceted approach which Mederi designed themselves. Yance has been working with oncologists all over the world using his approach which combines an emphasis on enhancing one's spirit, the use of botanicals in a strict dietary program, along with the use of mainstream treatments. It is my belief that the Lord led me to these great people through an underground alliance from Savannah, Georgia.

At the time of the writing of this book, it is 2015. I have changed cancer treatment protocols with my current oncologist and I am one of two people in the region using Kadycla. I have been living now for two years on this new protocol. On this targeted therapy, almost 98 percent of the side effects of the previous therapies are gone. I look and feel like a normal person. I have all my hair, my nail color has changed from black to normal. No more hot flashes, my energy level is good, and my blood work has improved. I can exercise, and I have little to no neuropathy. I have no nausea and have no shortness of breath. My marker levels remain in the normal range and my monitoring PET scans are stable. I have lost 24 pounds and am in overall good health. *Praise the Lord. Hallelujah!*

Like many patients, I have wondered about the unknown. Yes, even though I have great faith, and I am firm in my belief that ***The Grace of God is Sufficient***, I

know that I am very vulnerable at this stage in telling my story. I know the enemy is mad and doesn't want you encouraged, he doesn't want you informed, he wants you faithless and hopeless. So as I close, I will end by thanking all my loved ones and friends for their continued support over the course of this journey. I also want to thank the prophet for having me sit down and focus to write this book. In the interim, I will end with a prayer for you if you are going through cancer or if you are the supporter of someone who is going through cancer. Remember, no matter what, "Trust God in life and in death. Trust him with tumors or without. Just accept your healing in your speech, attitude and in how you walk. This honors God. He is faithful to show himself true. **Go forth my friends and live!!!**

Father, in the name of Jesus, Hear my prayer for your people. Lord, let not your children fear the dreaded call of cancer or disease. I thank you Lord that your children are full of courage and full of faith. Help them to see that your grace is all that they need, ***for Your Grace is Sufficient****. I pray that each person will place his/her full trust in you, no matter what type of report is given to him or her.*

Lord, remind your children of their rights and the benefit of healing they have in you. I pray that each person and loved one will join in agreement, knowing that you will supply everything for them. Place in your children a fierce spirit of determination to serve you, to believe in you. May your saints first believe that your Word is divinely inspired and true. Secondly, may your saints act out their faith in word and in deed. And lastly, may your saints walk in the full hope in you, when there seems to be no hope.

We thank you Lord for our lives. Show us Lord, your perfect will and equip us to do it. Let no weapon formed against us, prosper. Continue to cover us with your wings in healing. Command your angels to lift us up, so that our feet do not hit up against the stone. Let no harm befall us Lord, in the name of Jesus.

We love you Lord and will continue to give you 100 percent credit for everything. For all the glory belongs to you. Let no doubt or fear enter the minds of our loved ones. I thank you Lord that your people are on one accord, in perfect peace with your Word. We believe what you say, and believe we will receive what you have for us.

Now Lord, strengthen our health care providers, have them walk by and in faith as well. We pray for our doctors and medical community. Increase their intellect and heart as we know their talent comes from you. Come against the ills of greed, ignorance and malfeasance within our healthcare system and protect your people from the wiles of the enemy.

I thank you Lord for all that you have done, and I thank you Lord in advance for all you will do in the future.

Amen

Healing and Hope Scriptures
(Feel free to remove these pages and carry with you)

1) I shall live and shall not die, and will declare the works of the Lord. ***(Psalms 118:17)***

2) But He was wounded for our transgressions, He was bruised for our iniquities; The chastisement for our peace was upon Him, And by His stripes we are healed. ***(Isaiah 53:5)***

*3) When he heard this, Jesus said, "This sickness will not end in death. No, it is for God's glory so that God's Son may be glorified through it.****(John 11:4)***

4) O LORD my God, I cried out to You, And You healed me. ***(Psalms 30:2)***

5) Bless the LORD, O my soul; And all that is within me, bless His holy name!

Bless the LORD, O my soul, And forget not all His benefits:

Who forgives all your iniquities, Who heals all your diseases,

Who redeems your life from destruction, Who crowns you with loving kindness and tender mercies. ***(Psalms 103:1-4)***

6) He sent His word and healed them, And delivered them from their destructions. ***(Psalms 107:20)***

7) Heal me, O LORD, and I shall be healed; Save me, and I shall be saved, For You are my praise. ***(Jeremiah 17:14)***

8) "For I will restore health to you And heal you of your wounds," says the LORD, 'Because they called you an outcast saying: 'This is Zion; No one seeks her.'" ***(Jeremiah 30:17)***

9) Lord You are my Jehovah Rapha. My God Who Heals…

10) Beloved, I pray that in all things thou may prosper and be in health, even as thy soul prosperity. **(3John 1:2)**

11) A merry heart doeth good like a medicine! **(Proverbs 17:22)**

12) The thief cometh not, but for to steal, and to kill, and to destroy: I am come that they might have life, and that they might have it more abundantly. **(John 10:10)**

13) And He has said to me, "My grace is sufficient for you, for power is perfected in weakness." Most gladly, therefore, I will rather boast about my weaknesses, so that the power of Christ may dwell in me. **(2 Corinthians 12:9**)

*14) Be strong and courageous. Do not be afraid or terrified because of them, for the LORD your God goes with you; he will never leave you nor forsake you.***(Deut 31:6)**

15) Peace I leave with you; my peace I give you. I do not give to you as the world gives. Do not let your hearts be troubled and do not be afraid. **(John 14:27**)

16)Do not let your hearts be troubled. You believe in God; believe also in me. **(John 14:1)**

*17) I have told you these things, so that in me you may have peace. In this world you will have trouble. But take heart! I have overcome the world.***(John 16:33)**

.18) Now faith is the substance of things hoped for and the evidence of things not seen. **(Hebrews 11:1**)

19)....No calamity or harm will overtake me. **(Psalms 91:10**)

20) No ill befalls the righteous, but the wicked are filled with trouble. **(Proverbs 12:21**)

21) He will command his angels concerning you, to guard you carefully. (**Luke 4:10**)

22) ....Command your angels to lift me up so my foot does not hit up against a stone. (**Psalms 91:11)**

23)...No weapon formed against me shall prosper. (**Isaiah 54:17**)

24) Do not be anxious about anything, but in everything by prayer and supplication with thanksgiving, let your requests be made known to God. (**Philippians 4:6)**

25) So be strong and courageous! Do not be afraid and do not panic before them. For the Lord your God will personally go ahead of you. He will neither fail you, nor abandon you. (**Deuteronomy 31:6)**

About the Author

Shatrece W. Buchanan, Retired Army Lieutenant Colonel, CEO of Eagle Talon, Inc. and Pastor of Eagle Talon Faith & Vision Center

LTC Buchanan is a dynamic communicator who inspires through her testimony as a 5X survivor of cancer. She is a proven leader and visionary of 24 years in the Armed Forces, 19 years as a leader of a Christian production company and bible study teaching ministry. She is the author of numerousstage plays, book derivatives and now "A 5X Cancer Survivor".

She is married to Harvey G. Buchanan, Jr. and lives in North Florida.

Shatrece is available for speaking engagements to tell her dynamic testimony of how God's Grace has made her whole.

Email her at shatrece5@yahoo.com or

log onto her website at

www.eagletalon.org to contact her or to purchase a book.

Made in the USA
Charleston, SC
09 June 2016